THE
RISE OF
REASON

The History of SCIENCE

THE
RISE OF
REASON

1700–1799

Ray Spangenburg
Diane Kit Moser

☑® Facts On File, Inc.

The Rise of Reason: 1700–1799

Facts On File, Inc.
132 West 31st Street
New York NY 10001

Library of Congress Cataloging-in-Publication Data

Spangenburg, Ray, 1939–
    The rise of reason: 1700–1799 / Ray Spangenburg and Diane Kit Moser.
        p. cm. — (The history of science)
Rev. ed. of: History of science in the eighteenth century. 1993.
Summary: Discusses major scientists and scientific issues and discoveries of the eighteenth and early nineteenth centuries.
    ISBN 0-8160-4852-5
    1. Science—History—18th century. [1. Science—History—18th century.] I. Moser, Diane, 1944– II. Spangenburg, Ray, 1939– History of science in the eighteenth century. III. Title.
    Q126.4.S65 2004
    509'.033—dc22   2003019471

Facts On File books are available at special discounts when purchased in bulk quantities for businesses, associations, institutions, or sales promotions. Please call our Special Sales Department in New York at (212) 967-8800 or (800) 322-8755.

You can find Facts On File on the World Wide Web at http://www.factsonfile.com

Text design by Erika K. Arroyo
Cover design by Nora Wertz
Illustrations by Sholto Ainslie

Printed in the United States of America

MP Hermitage 10 9 8 7 6 5 4 3 2 1

This book is printed on acid-free paper.

In Memory of
Morgan Sherwood
and his love of the ever–human
struggle to become rational

CONTENTS

PREFACE

What I see in Nature is a magnificent structure that we can comprehend only very imperfectly, and that must fill a thinking person with a feeling of "humility."

—Albert Einstein

SCIENCE, OF ALL HUMAN ENDEAVORS, is one of the greatest adventures: Its job is to explore that "magnificent structure" we call nature and its awesome unknown regions. It probes the great mysteries of the universe such as black holes, star nurseries, and quasars, as well as the perplexities of miniscule subatomic particles, such as quarks and antiquarks. Science seeks to understand the secrets of the human body and the redwood tree and the retrovirus. The realms of its inquiry embrace the entire universe and everything in it, from the smallest speck of dust on a tiny asteroid to the fleck of color in a girl's eye, and from the vast structure of a far-off galaxy millions of light years away to the complex dynamics that keep the rings of Saturn suspended in space.

Some people tend to think that science is a musty, dusty set of facts and statistics to be memorized and soon forgotten. Others contend that science is the antithesis of poetry, magic, and all things human. Both groups have it wrong—nothing could be more growth-oriented or more filled with wonder or more human. Science is constantly evolving, undergoing revolutions, always producing "new words set to the old music," and constantly refocusing what has gone before into fresh, new understanding.

Asking questions and trying to understand how things work are among the most fundamental of human characteristics, and the history of science is the story of how a varied array of individuals,

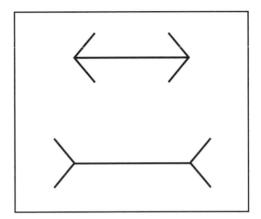

Looks can be deceiving. These two lines are the same length.

teams, and groups have gone about finding answers to some of the most fundamental questions. When, for example, did people begin wondering what Earth is made of and what its shape might be? How could they find answers? What methods did they devise for coming to conclusions and how good were those methods? At what point did their inquiries become *scientific*—and what does that mean?

Science is so much more than the strange test tubes and odd apparatus we see in movies. It goes far beyond frog dissections or the names of plant species that we learn in biology classes. Science is actually a way of thinking, a vital, ever-growing way of looking at the world. It is a way of discovering how the world works—a very particular way that uses a set of rules devised by scientists to help them also discover their own mistakes because it is so easy to misconstrue what one sees or hears or perceives in other ways.

If you find that hard to believe, look at the two horizontal lines in the figure above. One looks like a two-way arrow; the other has inverted arrowheads. Which one do you think is longer (not including the "arrowheads")? Now measure them both. Right, they are exactly the same length. Because it is so easy to go wrong in making observations and drawing conclusions, people developed a system, a "scientific method," for asking "How can I be sure?" If you actually took the time to measure the two lines in our example, instead of just taking our word that both lines are the same length, then you were thinking like a scientist. You were testing your own observation. You were testing the information that both lines "are exactly the same length." And you were employing one of the strongest tools of science to perform your test: You were quantifying, or measuring, the lines.

More than 2,300 years ago, Aristotle, a Greek philosopher, told the world that when two objects of different weights were dropped from a height, the heaviest would hit the ground first. It was a commonsense argument. After all, anyone who wanted to try a test could make an "observation" and see that if you dropped a leaf and a stone together that the stone would land first. Try it yourself with a sheet of notebook paper and a paperweight in your living room. (There is something wrong with this test. Do you know what it is?) However, not many Greek thinkers tried any sort of test. Why bother when the answer was already known? And, since they were philosophers who believed in the power of the human mind to simply "reason" such things out without having to resort to "tests," they considered observation and experiments intellectually and socially beneath them.

Centuries later, though, Galileo Galilei came along, a brilliant Italian pioneer in physics and telescopic astronomy. Galileo liked to figure things out for himself, and he did run some tests, even though he had to work around some limitations. Like today's scientists, Galileo was never content just to watch. He used two balls of different weights, a time-keeping device, and an inclined plane, or ramp. Accurate clocks and watches were not yet invented, but he worked around that problem by rigging his own device. One at a time, he allowed the balls to roll down the ramp and carefully *measured* the time they took to reach the end of the ramp. He did this not once but many times, inclining planes at many different angles. His results, which still offend the common sense of many people today, indicated that, in Aristotle's example, after adjusting for differences in air resistance, all objects released at the same time from the same height would hit the ground at the same time. In a perfect vacuum (which scientists could not create in Galileo's time), all objects would fall at the same rate! You can run a rough test yourself (although it is by no means a really accurate experiment) by crumpling notebook paper into a ball and then dropping it at the same time as the paperweight.

"Wait!" you might justifiably say. Just a minute ago, you dropped a piece of paper and a paperweight and so demonstrated Aristotle's premise when the two objects hit the ground at different times. Now when we do the same thing over again, the two objects hit the ground at about the same time and we demonstrate that Galileo was right and Aristotle was wrong. What makes the difference? You have it: The second time, you crumpled the paper so that it had the same shape as the paperweight. Without crumpling the paper, you would have to make an adjustment for the increased air resistance of an 8½-by-11-inch sheet of paper as opposed to a paperweight that had less surface area.

Galileo's experiments (which he carefully recorded step by step) and his conclusions based on these experiments demonstrate an important attribute of science. Anyone who wanted to could duplicate the experiments and either verify his results or, by showing flaws or errors in the experiments, prove him partially or wholly incorrect. Since his time, many, many scientists have repeated his experiment and, even though they tried, no one ever proved Galileo wrong. There is more. Years later, when it was possible to create a vacuum (even though his experiments had been accurate enough to win everybody over long before that), his prediction proved true. Without any air resistance at all and even with much more sophisticated timing devices, his experiment came out as predicted.

Galileo had not only shown that Aristotle had been wrong. He demonstrated how, by observation, experiment, and quantification, Aristotle, if he had so wished, might have proved himself wrong—and thus changed his own opinion! Above all else the scientific way of thinking is a way to keep yourself from fooling yourself—or from letting nature (or others) fool you.

Of course, science is much more than observation, experimentation, and presentation of results. No one today can read a newspaper or a magazine without becoming quickly aware of the fact that science is always bubbling with "theories." "Astronomer Finds Evidence That Challenges Einstein's Theory of Relativity," announces a magazine cover. "State Board of Education Condemns Books That Teach Darwin's Theory of Evolution," reads a newspaper headline. What is this thing called a "theory"? The answer lies in a process known as the "scientific method."

Few scientists pretend anymore that they have the completely "detached" and objective scientific method proposed by the philosopher Francis Bacon and others at the dawn of the Scientific Revolution in the 17th century. Bacon's method, in its simplest form, proposed that an investigator trying to find out about nature's secrets had an obligation to think objectively and proceed without preformed opinions, basing conclusions on observation, experiments, and collection of data about the phenomena under inquiry. "I make no hypothesis," Isaac Newton announced after demonstrating the universal law of gravity when it was suggested that he might have an idea *what gravity was*. Historians have noted that Newton apparently did have a couple of ideas, or "hypotheses," as to the possible nature of gravity, but for the most part he kept these conjectures private. As far as Newton was concerned, there had already been enough hypothesizing and too little attention paid to the careful gathering of testable facts and figures.

Today, though, we know that scientists may not always follow along the simple and neat pathways laid out by the trail guide known as the "scientific method." Sometimes, either before or after experiments, a scientist will get an idea or a hunch (that is, a somewhat less than well thought out hypothesis) that suggests a new approach or a different way of looking at a problem. Then the researcher will run experiments and gather data to attempt to prove or disprove this hypothesis. Sometimes the word *hypothesis* is used loosely in everyday conversation, but in science it must meet an important requirement: To be valid scientifically a hypothesis must have a built-in way it can be proved wrong if, in fact, it is wrong. That is, it must be falsifiable.

Not all scientists actually run experiments themselves. Most theoreticians, for instance, map out their arguments mathematically. But hypotheses, to be taken seriously by the scientific community, must always carry with them the seeds of falsifiability by experiment and observation.

That brings us to the word *theory*. To become a theory, a hypothesis has to pass several tests. It has to hold up under repeated experiments and not done just by one scientist. Other scientists, working separately from the first, must also perform experiments and observations to test the hypothesis. Then, when thoroughly reinforced by continual testing and appraising, the hypothesis may become known to the scientific and popular world as a "theory."

It is important to remember that even a theory is also subject to falsification or correction. A good theory, for instance, will suggest "predictions"—events that its testers can look for as further tests of its validity. By the time most well-known theories, such as Einstein's theory of relativity or Darwin's theory of evolution, reach the textbook stage, they have survived the gamut of verification to the extent that they have become productive working tools for other scientists. But in science, no theory can be accepted as completely "proved"; it must remain always open to further tests and scrutiny as new facts or observations emerge. It is this insistently self-correcting nature of science that makes it both the most demanding and the most productive of humankind's attempts to understand the workings of nature. This kind of critical thinking is the key element of doing science.

The cartoon-version scientist, portrayed as a bespectacled, rigid man in a white coat and certain of his own infallibility, couldn't be further from reality. Scientists, both men and women, are as human as the rest of us—and they come in all races, sizes, and appearances, with and without eyeglasses. As a group, because their methodology focuses so specifically on fallibility and critical thinking, they are probably even more aware than the rest of us of how easy it is to be wrong. But they like being right whenever possible, and they like working toward finding the right answers to questions. That's usually why they became scientists.

The Rise of Reason: 1700–1799 and the four other volumes in The History of Science look at how people have developed this system for finding out how the world works, making use of both success and failure. Throughout the series, we look at the theories scientists have put forth, sometimes right and sometimes wrong. And we look at how we have learned to test, accept, and build upon those theories—or to correct, expand, or simplify them.

We also examine how scientists have learned from others' mistakes, sometimes having to discard theories that once seemed logical but later proved to be incorrect, misleading, too limited, or unfruitful. In all these ways they have built upon the accomplishments of the men and women of science who went before them and left a long, bountiful legacy from which others could set out for new discoveries and fresh insights.

Each volume of this new edition offers expanded coverage, including more about women in science; many new photographs and illustrations; and a new section, "Science and Society" that examines the interface between science and cultural and social mores and historical events. Sidebars called "Side Roads of Science" examine weird beliefs and pseudoscientific claims of the times. Each volume concludes with a glossary, a chronology, and expanded sources for further exploration, including Web sites, CD-ROMs, and other multimedia resources, as well as recent related books and other print resources.

ACKNOWLEDGMENTS

WE COULD NOT HAVE WRITTEN this book or the others in this series without the help, inspiration, and guidance offered by many generous individuals over nearly two decades of writing about science and science history. We would like to name a few of them; for those we have not space to name please accept our heartfelt thanks, including the many scientists we have interviewed. Their work has helped us better understand the overall nature of science.

We would like to express our heartfelt appreciation to James Warren, formerly of Facts On File, whose vision and enthusiastic encouragement helped shape the first edition; Frank K. Darmstadt, executive editor, whose boundless energy and support made all this book and its companions happen against impossible odds; and all the rest of the Facts On File staff. A special thank you as well to Heather Lindsay of AIP Emilio Segrè Visual Archives, Lynne Farrington of the Annenberg Rare Book and Manuscript Library, Tracy Elizabeth Robinson and David Burgevin of the Smithsonian, and Shirley Neiman of Stock Montage, Inc. Our heartfelt gratitude also to Frances Spangenburg, even though she will never read this one, for her unflagging encouragement at every step of our writing careers.

And finally, our gratitude and affection to the late Morgan Sherwood and his wife, Jeanie Sherwood, for their warmth and generosity and their gift of Morgan's fine, extensive library on pseudoscience and the history of science.

INTRODUCTION

BY THE END OF THE 17TH CENTURY, scientists had staged a successful rebellion against slavish acceptance of ancient and medieval authorities—despite their stature. With new and rebellious enthusiasm, scientists had toppled Ptolemy in astronomy, Galen in physiology, and Aristotle in astronomy, physics, and nearly all the other sciences. Their rebellion became known eventually as the Scientific Revolution, and the rebels eagerly reexamined every precept with skepticism and measured every assumption with the new standards of reason, observation, experiment, and mathematics.

The 18th century dawned with a confidence that the world was getting better—and the confidence had a name: the doctrine of progress. It was a time of enormous excitement and vigor, a time of exciting discoveries in all the sciences, including physics, astronomy, geology, and biology. Important insights about gases and their properties transformed chemistry from its marginal "cooking" traditions and its ties to magic and alchemy to become a true science. Astronomy's ever-improving instruments fostered both solar system and deep-sky discoveries. Cooperative international expeditions made possible measurements of the Earth and calculations of the size of the solar system. It was a time when brilliant, energetic individuals envisioned and produced a giant work known as the *Encyclopédie ou dictionnaire raisonné des sciences, des arts et des métiers* (Encyclopedia or systematic dictionary of sciences, arts, and trades), or just the *Encyclopédie,* which would set out to detail all human knowledge of the time.

Oddly, in the midst of all this fervor and excitement, for some scientists the future seemed laid out in such a highly structured, predictable order that the scientific process itself seemed mundane and unexciting. Gone was the rebellious excitement (and suffering) experienced by Galileo, Descartes, and Newton—and others who led the vanguard for the new methodology of observation and experiment. No one gave credence any more to the old authorities. That battle had been won. All that remained was to follow the template.

Similarly, for many nonscientists today, science and reason have taken on a tarnished hue. A broad-based disenchantment with science permeates much popular thinking, along with an unsettling distrust of scientists. Scientists have become the scapegoats for political decisions about the use of inventions and knowledge gained from science. Science has provided us with deadly weapons that have enormous destructive power, capable of destroying the planet we live on and annihilating entire populations. The impact of our technology—for example, the emissions of our automobiles—has begun to show wear and tear on Earth's fragile environment. We no longer naively believe that science can solve everything.

Moreover, a blighting approach to literature known as postmodernism has extended its application beyond literary criticism to a worldview held in both university and popular circles across academic disciplines and national boundaries. Postmodernism questions whether we can ever arrive at real knowledge, placing its tenets in direct opposition to science and rational approaches to understanding the universe, our planet, and everything around and within us. In anthropology postmodernists take the defensible view that people are constantly creating culture and that culture is a shifting process of change and adaptation and reinterpretation. Inasmuch as this is true of all things human, postmodernism provides a useful description of the evolving processes of human life and development of culture. French philosopher Jacques Derrida has taken this same tenet and applied it to literature through the use of a critical technique known as *deconstruction*. A deconstructionist critic assumes a world where nothing is knowable. Everything is open to multiple interpretations and all conflicts of interpretation are impossible to resolve. Language has boundless capabilities for signifying meaning, and no single meaning can ever be assigned to anything. The philosophy of deconstructionism stems from 19th-century philosopher Friedrich Nietzsche's abhorrence of the domination and mystification stemming from the misuses of language, but it effectively destroys any hope of communicating effectively or clearly.

Further, the legacy of postmodernism and desconstructionism leaves the public without the tools to frame opinions, delineate values, and pursue understanding. Because attempts at understanding are seen as useless, people are disenfranchised. The premises of deconstruction have become dogma for many college graduates and have permeated the thinking of the public at large. Since these premises are the antithesis of the processes of science and rational thinking, many people tend to see science as cut and dried, lacking in mystery and beauty, and out of step with the complexities of life.

Nothing could be further from reality. Science is a celebration of the mysteries of the universe. Scientists thrive on the complexities of nature and life—and the more they peel the outer layers off the onion of reality, the more they find to explore. Their goal is to find the next layer of complexities to understand, to find the new relationships exposed by looking ever further below the surface.

So now is the perfect time for an exploration of the Enlightenment and the men and women of the 18th century who probed and tested and observed in ever-new ways to discover what made the world tick. The fascinating story of their trials and missteps—such as the phlogiston theory of why things burn, which did not hit the mark—illustrates the self-correcting nature of science. The stories of their newly devised tests for gases; advances in temperature measurement; improvements in the language of chemistry; discoveries about the stars, planets, and comets; and the classification of living things— all these stories and more illustrate both the usefulness and the fascination of their work. These were unique, exciting times to live in, when human rights, fair government, and individualism were replacing old, despotic regimes. The Industrial Revolution dramatically changed the potentials for productivity (along with many abuses that had to be overcome, admittedly). Optimism permeated the philosophy of these scientists and also the outlook of many political leaders and much of the populace. Though naive, their confidence and enthusiasm are exhilarating and infectious, and their celebration of the human mind, human dignity, and the thirst for knowledge is an inspiration for our own time. These were men and women who believed in improvement and growth, the giants of 18th-century science, and their lives and work have a story to tell for readers of all ages—especially for those just embarking upon their careers.

Like the four other books in The History of Science series, *The Rise of Reason* looks at the development of science through an examination of the men and women who shaped its history. In this volume, we examine how the scientists of the 18th century extended the methods of science, developing a process that helped them see nature in all its guises more clearly and to build an understanding of the universe around them. Their progress, though exciting, was not always sure, as you will see as we follow the fascinating side road of the phlogiston theory. The story reflects the many different temperaments of its cast of characters—the flamboyant showmanship of Georges Cuvier, the eccentric style of Henry Cavendish, the sparkling wit and ego of Antoine Lavoisier—and his tragic end, the lonely persistence of Linnaeus, the confident brilliance of Laura Bassi, and more. This is the exciting story of science at work.

For exploring related topics, a bibliography at the end of this volume provides Internet addresses, multimedia references, and an updated list of books reflecting recent research and interpretations, as well as a few classics. A chronology and glossary round out the reference tools at the conclusion of the volume.

PART I

The Physical Sciences in the 18th Century

1

Exploring the New Solar System

PEOPLE HAVE ALWAYS LOOKED FOR knowledge in various ways, delving for explanations and searching their world for answers. They have also always used the richness of their minds—their imaginations and their faith—to bridge what seemed impossible to understand. From the beginning of time they have told stories of gods and superhuman men and women who forged the forces that made the world work, the Sun rise, the rains come, and the harvests grow. Shamans and priests fashioned rituals by which they sought to control pestilence and disease and drive away drought.

However, from earliest times, human beings have also used their powers of observation and calculations. Very early, people in several areas of the world—including China and the Mesopotamian basin—began to develop the tools of mathematics, language, and writing. They also developed more quantitative and objective approaches for describing phenomena and devising explanations. By 1800 B.C.E. the Sumerians in the Middle East and the Babylonians, who succeeded them, had made many accurate observations about the stars and planets and had developed numerical systems and ways to keep records. Cuneiform and pictograph writing systems began even earlier, and by 1300 B.C.E. the Phoenicians had alphabets based on earlier systems developed by the Egyptians and the Babylonians. By the time of the ancient Greeks in the last four or five centuries B.C.E., analytical methods, logic, and geometry began to be finely honed. Several Greek thinkers, in particular, began to explore more nonmystical explanations. Aristotle (384–322 B.C.E.), perhaps the greatest of the Greek thinkers, also devised the first integrated natural theory about

3

how the universe worked, with intricate visions of nested spheres that held the planets and the stars and circled around the Earth. Clarifications and improvements were contributed by several followers, including a thinker named Ptolemy (ca. 100–ca. 170 C.E.) who lived in Alexandria, Egypt, a few centuries later.

Greek ideas about mathematics, philosophy, and science reigned supreme up to the fall of the Roman Empire, when many manuscripts were burned by invading tribes as they sacked the cities in their paths. Some, however, were preserved, largely by Islamic scholars and later passed into hands of monks in the monasteries of Europe. Partly as a result of this preservation and partly because no one questioned it, Aristotle's concept of a universe composed of concentric spheres revolving around the Earth—augmented by Ptolemy—remained the best explanation of the cosmos anyone came up with for 14 centuries.

Then, in a daring sweep of imagination, the Polish theorist Nicolaus Copernicus revised that theory in the 16th century by placing the Sun, not the Earth, at the center of the circling planets. Called the Copernican system, this Sun-centered view of the solar system (and, actually, the universe at the time) turned every doctrine and assumption about the world and humanity's place in it upside down. When two more great astronomers, the Danish observer Tycho Brahe (1546–1601) and his one-time assistant from Germany, Johannes Kepler (1571–1630), added their own observations and calculations to verify Copernicus's ideas, most people thought they, too, were heretics. When the Italian astronomer Galileo Galilei (1564–1642) defended the idea in his book *Dialogue on the Two Chief Systems of the World,* published in 1632, he was tried by the Catholic Church and his book was banned—put on the Index—where it stayed until 1835. (Not until 1992, in fact, did the pope formally declare that Galileo was right.) Even though careful inquiry and reasoning supported Copernicus's idea, a Sun-centered solar system did not make sense if one took certain passages of the Bible literally. Theologians and their followers pointed significantly to the Old Testament story in which God stopped the movements of the Sun across the sky so that the people led by Joshua could win a crucial battle. The Sun, then, must be moving around the Earth and not vice versa, readers reasoned. To resolve the conflict between nature observed and the Bible's authority, church authorities recommended keeping faith with the Bible rather than revise biblical interpretation as Galileo's views would require. Church doctrine also maintained that humanity was created in God's image and that therefore God would not have created the universe in a way that did not revolve around the Earth. So a battle raged between those who wanted to rely on human ability to find things out through the use of the mind and the senses and those who preferred to depend on traditional authority for answers.

Nearly everyone today takes Copernicus's idea for granted that the Earth revolves around the Sun. (By now we have lots of scientific evidence to prove it.) But the stir his ideas caused in his time and in Galileo's time is a reminder of how hard it is to let go of old ways of thinking in the light of new facts. What made arguments for the Copernican system so powerful at the time, even against the spiritual and political strength of religion and tradition, was the birth of a new methodology, spawned in large part by the experimental work of Galileo. Scientists had come to recognize this methodology as extraordinarily effective for problem solving, and it soon became known as "the scientific method" (explained in more detail in the preface to this series).

Scientific method calls for explanations based on observation and collected facts and measurements—not on reasoning alone or on emotional reactions, visions, hearsay, or faith. The scientific method accepts only explanations that can be verified over and over by experiments. The results of these experiments, summarized in theories, can then be used to make predictions about other phenomena not yet observed. Then when the opportunity arises to test one of these predictions, the results of that test can be compared with the predicted results. In this way the results of experiments and observations are constantly used to modify existing theories—which is what makes science a "self-correcting" process. This fundamental change in the way people looked at the world, which took place in the period just preceding the first years covered in this book, is commonly referred to as the Scientific Revolution.

Many of the most important scientific discoveries in the 17th century had centered in Italy. Even Copernicus had trained there in astronomy in the 1500s, and while Tycho and Kepler had also come from the more northern regions of Denmark and Germany, the great names in the life sciences either trained in Italy or were born there. Among the many notable scientists of the period who studied life sciences in Italy are Andreas Vesalius (1514–64), the Flemish founder of human anatomy; William Harvey (1578–1657), the English physician who made breakthrough progress in the area of blood circulation; and Marcello Malpighi (1628–94), the Italian physiologist who discovered capillaries in frogs' lungs.

By the end of the century, though, the focus of growth had begun to sift north to France and England. In England especially, economic dependence on far-flung colonies in North America, Africa, and Asia created an urgent need for reliable knowledge about navigation. The English government—understanding that knowledge of the stars and their positions was the key to navigation—created the position of Astronomer Royal, and John Flamsteed (1646–1719) was appointed to the post. Edmond Halley (1656–1742), Christopher Wren (1632–1723), and Robert Hooke (1635–1703), among others, formed a society of scientists called the Royal Society in 1662. (Its motto, *Nullius in Verba*—take nobody's word, or see for yourself—set the stage for the next century.) The greatest of all English scientists, Isaac Newton, became a member

In addition to his landmark work on gravity and the laws of motion, Isaac Newton studied light and optics. In this image, the artist shows Newton experimenting with light, demonstrating that sunlight can be broken down into its components, or colors, by shining the light through a prism. *(Louis Figuier:* Vies des savants illustres du dix-huitième siècle, *vol. V, 1870)*

of the society in 1671, and in 1687 he published a book called *Principia mathematica* that synthesized the ideas of the Scientific Revolution and set forth basic principles of the universe, "laws" of motion that nature followed.

In what are now known as Newton's three laws of motion, the great English synthesizer mathematically demonstrated principles that Galileo explored with some of his experiments:

1. the principle of inertia (a body at rest remains at rest and a body in motion remains in motion at a constant velocity as long as outside forces are not involved);
2. definition of a force in terms of mass and acceleration; and
3. the famous statement that for every action there is an equal and opposite reaction (the principle that governs the behavior of rockets).

By the beginning of the 18th century, the work of such intellectual giants as Galileo and Newton and others had revolutionized science and the acquisition of knowledge. These thinkers had established a new way of perceiving nature and had forever altered humanity's understanding of itself and the universe.

One of the exciting peculiarities of science is that every new theory produces new questions and casts new light on old ones. The better the theory, the more fruitful the questions it raises. The theories contained in Newton's *Principia mathematica* were no exception. The French in particular felt uneasy about this force called gravity that Newton claimed was the universal explanation of motion in the cosmos and on Earth. What was the precise nature of gravity? Newton himself could not say. Was it a force inherent in physical objects? To this query, Newton replied, "Pray do not ascribe that notion to me." The French thought this sounded a trifle medieval and referred to Newton's theories as the "metaphysical monster." (We still do not completely understand gravity, although when Einstein described it in the 20th century as the result of curvatures in space, it became more comprehensible.)

Partly to try to settle some of these questions, early in the 18th century the scientific community—especially the Royal Society in England and the newly formed French Academy of Sciences— became ablaze with two intriguing questions brought into focus by Newton and the Scientific Revolution: (1) What is the true shape of Earth? (2) How far away is the Sun? Both questions prompted a series of exciting expeditions whose scientific inspiration was completely unprecedented in history.

The Battle of the Bulge

Newton had predicted, based on his theories of gravity, that Earth's shape would not be a perfect sphere as the ancient Greeks had thought.

Instead, Newton proclaimed, our planet would bulge at the equator and be flattened at the poles by various gravitational forces, such as the pull of the Sun and the Moon. Not only did Newton's prediction present a way to test his theory, but this fairly abstract idea also had practical implications for people trying to travel in those days—especially those navigating at sea. If Newton was right, all the world's maps were wrong. For the English the matter seemed urgent: The answers, once found, would not only prove or disprove Newton's theory, they would also either transform or reinforce current navigation procedures. The great flurry of voyages and expeditions that followed was rivaled in history only by the search for the Indies and the discovery of America during the age of Columbus and Magellan. In fact these and other scientific questions inspired such intense interest and so much activity that historian William H. Goetzmann has called this period the "Second Great Age of Discovery."

Actually the question of Earth's shape had been in the air for some time—since this was not the first mention Newton made of this idea. So by 1700 the "oblate spheroid" (another way of describing a flattened globe) had become highly controversial, part of an international feud between England and France. On one side was Giovanni Cassini (1625–1712), who was then the director of the Paris Observatory (enticed away from his native Italy by Louis XIV of France). Cassini provided a powerful conservative voice in French astronomy, passing on both his conservatism and his position at the observatory to members of his family for three generations. Cassini not only rejected Nicolaus Copernicus's Sun-centered universe but also threw his influence behind the cosmic view of René Descartes [day-KART] (1596–1650), a rival to Newton who saw the Earth carried around the Sun in a swirling vortex, in a sort of whirlpool of subtle matter. At rest in the center of the vortex, according to Descartes, the planet Earth was motionless, as it was carried in orbit by the motion of the vortex around it. To many his idea made more sense than Newton's "mystery force" that he could not explain, and as a result, in France, followers of Descartes, including Cassini, maintained that Earth was the shape of a "prolate spheroid," elongated at the poles (the shape of an American football).

In part to prove this point, Jean Richer [ree-SHAY] (1630–96), an associate of Cassini's, set out in 1671 for the town of Cayenne, located very near the equator, in French Guiana on the northern shore of South America. There, coordinating with Cassini in Paris, he performed a series of experiments and observations, among them an exact measurement of the length of a pendulum required to tick off one second of time. To Cassini's amazement the pendulum in Cayenne was shorter, not longer, than the one in Paris (990 mm, as opposed to 994 mm). He refused to accept the results and repudiated his former friend. Newton, however, contended that these measurements showed the force of gravity at the equator to be weaker than at the poles, which would be expected if the Earth bulged at the equator.

By this time Descartes's opposing view became a national cause among French scientists, and proving it true became a point of honor. Cassini and Jean Picard [pee-KAHR] (1620–82) had led the way by establishing the distance in one degree of latitude, based on the prolate spheroid theory. From that start they began figuring the path of longitude through Paris to the two "ends of the Earth." Also French cartographers were working on the definitive scientific map of their nation.

By the 1730s, though, Newton's theories became popular in France through the writings of Voltaire—whose sharp wit had earned him several years' exile in England—and thanks to translations of Newton's work from Latin into French by Voltaire's friend and lover, Emilie du Châtelet [shah-TLAY]. The French Academy of Sciences decided to settle the question of the shape of the Earth once and for all by measuring the curvature of the planet at widely separated locations, as close as possible to the equator and the north pole, where Newton's predictions should be most apparent. Two expeditions were organized, one heading south in 1735 for Peru, and the other departing a year later for Lapland, far to the north.

Led by Pierre de Maupertuis [moh-pair-TWEE], the Lapland expedition included several illustrious scientists, among them Anders Celsius, a noted astronomer from Uppsala, Sweden, and Alexis-Claude Clairaut [klar-OH], a brilliant French mathematician, who had published his first book on math at the age of 10 and was

As part of a cooperative effort organized by the Paris Academy of Science, Pierre-Louis-Moreau de Maupertuis led a party of scientists and technicians to Lapland in 1736–37 to help measure the shape of the Earth. *(Figuier,* Vies des savants, *1870)*

admitted into the Academy of Sciences at the age of 18. Maupertuis, a respected French physicist, had visited England in 1728, shortly after Newton's death. There the Royal Society had elected Maupertuis to membership and he had become a great enthusiast of Newton's work, which he promoted eagerly on his return to France. He was delighted with this opportunity to head a scientific journey to prove Newton's theory of universal gravitation and rescue it from the nationalistic controversy in which it had become entangled.

Maupertuis's party set off in 1736 to face numerous hardships in the cold, barren lands of the north, including a near shipwreck in the Baltic Sea. They braved freezing rapids and slept in reindeer skins on the hard, rocky ground, subsisting on wild berries and fish. Hampered by insects and fog they nonetheless succeeded in completing their measurements and returned triumphant to France in 1737. Their measurements, published in 1738, showed that the Earth was not a perfect sphere as the Greeks had supposed. Nor was it, for that matter, a prolate spheroid, as Descartes's followers had insisted. Instead it bulged slightly less at the poles than farther south. Maupertuis and his colleagues had proved Newton correct. The success, however, did not win Maupertuis great advancement in his career, perhaps because he had the misfortune to quarrel with the razor-tongued Voltaire, who sarcastically called him *le grand aplatisseur*—that is, the "great flattener."

Meanwhile the members of the expedition to Peru had embarked deep upon adventures of their own in the jungles and on the high Andean plains of South America. Led by 34-year-old Charles-Marie de La Condamine, an experienced scientist-adventurer, the Peruvian party spent 14 years trekking through steamy jungles and braving the heat and cold of windswept highlands in what has since become Ecuador. Maupertuis had left a year later, swept north, finished the job, and returned safely home a dozen years before the return of La Condamine's group. But his measurements were sketchier, less carefully and exactly completed, and for overall impact on 18th-century knowledge, La Condamine's trip outshone his colleague's.

La Condamine, who had studied mathematics and geodesy (the science of the shape and size of the Earth), had been elected in 1730 to the Academy of Sciences for his work measuring and mapping the coasts of Africa and Asia. Embarking in 1735 from La Rochelle, France, La Condamine and his crew sailed for Colombia and Panama, crossing the Isthmus and proceeding to the port of Manta. There his party split in two, with La Condamine heading 70 miles north with the hydrographer and mathematician Pierre Bouguer (who was of the Cassini school) to survey the first set of measurements along the equator. The rest of the party, which included both French and Spanish scientists, headed for the more southerly port of Guayaquil, the usual launching site for journeys to the town of Quito, located inland on the equator, high in the Andes. Once La Condamine and Bouguer had finished their measurements, Bouguer rejoined the rest of the party heading for Quito, while La Condamine journeyed with surveyor-scientist Pedro Maldonado, governor of Esmeralda, the province in which they were surveying. Traveling by dugout and accompanied by a group of boatmen who had escaped from a slave ship, the two scientists traveled a little-used route up the Esmeralda River to Quito. Surrounded by lush green jungle, hanging vines and diverse, exotic plant and animal life, La Condamine made note of every aspect of his experience. He found himself surrounded by the sounds and sights of a dense, complex world of unimaginable richness: brightly colored toucans, parrots, and tiny hummingbirds; chattering monkeys and stalking jaguars; crocodiles and tapirs. He encountered native people who used blowguns, and he took some of their poison back with him to Europe. He watched as jungle dwellers tapped the sap of the caoutchouc tree, noticed them molding the pliable substance into useful objects, and gathered samples of the first rubber to be introduced into Europe. In addition to his studies of mathematics, geodesy, and astronomy, he now found himself drawn into the worlds of natural history and anthropology, where his accurate powers of observation and attention to detail served these sciences as well.

Once La Condamine and Maldonado arrived in Quito, the task of measuring the Earth's curvature went slowly. Nervous politicians suspected the team of hunting for Incan treasures and misunderstood the pyramids of stone that they left as markers in their surveys. So La Condamine had to take time out to travel to Lima to gain

Women in Science: Laura Bassi, Physicist of Bologna

Laura Maria Caterina Bassi (1711–78), born in Bologna, Italy, was destined to become one of the first women in Western history to become a recognized physicist. Bassi's family placed a high value on education, and by age 20 she had gained recognition for her achievements in both Latin and philosophy. At that time she received four outstanding honors: The Academy of Sciences of Bologna awarded her a voting membership; she successfully defended 49 scientific and philosophical positions in a public debate in the Palazzo Pubblico; she obtained a doctorate in philosophy from the University of Bologna; and the following fall she received an appointment to the faculty of the University of Bologna.

Bologna was a relatively liberal city. Still, as a young, unmarried woman engaged in a traditionally male career, Bassi faced some discomfort from members of Bologna society. Meetings with fellow scientists were often awkward or impossible due to the close scrutiny of her activities by the community. This discomfort eased after her marriage to Giovanni Giuseppe Verati (1707–93), who was also a scientist. Verati's interests in medicine, anatomy, and uses of electricity in medicine served as a helpful complement to Bassi's training and background. Verati was highly supportive of his wife's career—even serving as her teaching assistant at permission for his team to complete their undertaking in peace. Finally they succeeded in tracing out a baseline along the high plains. Then they headed south, near Cuenca, where they completed their last measurement in March 1743.

From there La Condamine once again joined Maldonado to journey across the Andes to the Amazon River, traveling hundreds of miles along its course. La Condamine was the first European ever to introduce thorough observation into the exploration of that territory. Along the way he collected hundreds of botanical samples and continued the observations he had begun along the equator.

La Condamine and his group had taken several years longer to complete their tasks, but their expedition not only measured the shape of the Earth more carefully and accurately than the Lapland party had—providing firm confirmation for Newton—but they established a rich tradition of wide-ranging scientific expeditions,

one point. The couple also had eight children, or possibly 12, according to some reports.

Bassi's academic career benefited from the approval of family friends in high places—in the Senate in Rome (assuring the security of her teaching position at the University of Bologna) and in the Vatican (ensuring her foothold in the academic community). Outside Italy her work was recognized in both French- and English-speaking communities. However, given the prejudices and assumptions of the time, she probably could not have gained the forum in which to present her work without these sources of support. This gave her an edge over other women in her time who might have attempted to carve out a career in science, but the significant prowess of her abilities enabled her to take effective advantage of that edge.

Bassi's research resulted in five published papers and her teaching was highly acclaimed. In 1745 she received full membership in the Benedettini Academics, a prestigious group of scientists funded by the Vatican. In 1745 she became a member of the teaching faculty at the Collegio Montalto, and 10 years later she became professor of experimental physics at the Institute of Sciences at the University of Bologna, as well as co-chair of the department.

Laura Bassi died suddenly in 1778, just hours after participating in a lecture at the Academy of Sciences. She was 66.

long on perseverance and determination and even longer on accuracy and encyclopedic fact gathering of every kind.

The Transit of Venus and Captain James Cook

The question of the distance from Earth to the Sun inspired a second wave of expeditions even greater in number and intensity than those investigating Earth's shape.

From almost the beginning of time astronomers had tried to measure the distance of the Sun, the Moon, and the stars from Earth. But, because no direct method for measurement exists, the problem proved exceedingly difficult to solve. Two ancient Greeks, Aristarchus and Hipparchus, had tried, without any great success. (Aristarchus figured the Sun to be between 18 and 20 times more distant than the Moon, but in fact the distance is more like 340 times as far. Hipparchus was a little more in the ballpark but still very far off.) Not until Johannes Kepler (1571–1630) made some key discoveries about planetary orbits some 1,800 years later did anyone come up with a better method, though. Kepler realized that planets orbit the Sun in ellipses and that each planet's average distance from the Sun has a mathematical relationship to the time the planet takes to complete an orbit. So if one could determine the distance of a planet from Earth and observe how long the planet takes to orbit the Sun, then it would be possible to determine the distance to the Sun. Through the use of triangulation, a system of measurement based on trigonometry, it should be theoretically possible to determine the distance from the Earth to a nearby planet. Giovanni Domenico Cassini had tried in 1672 to use Mars for the calculation, using a telescope to measure the small angles. His figure for the distance of the Sun came far closer than anyone else's had before—86 million miles, as opposed to the distance we now know to be 93 million miles—but both the process and the results remained uncertain and frustrating.

Then Edmond Halley pointed out that Venus might be a far better candidate than Mars, since it approaches closer to Earth than Mars. But at its closest approach to Earth, Venus appears so close to the Sun that it cannot be observed at this time except on the rare occasions when it crosses the Sun's disk. This period of crossing, as seen from Earth, is known as a transit, and it is also sometimes referred to as an immersion because, to the observer, the planet seems immersed in the great, glowing globe of the Sun. Halley suggested in 1691 that such a transit would be a perfect opportunity to make measurements, simultaneously, from locations all over the Earth, timing from the moment the immersion begins and the planet appears outlined against the Sun's brilliance until it disappears again on the opposite side. But transits of Venus do not happen often. In fact they only occur in pairs separated by eight years, at intervals of more than 100 years. The next pair, they knew from orbital calculations, was not due to occur until 1761 and 1769. (The only transits of Venus in the 21st century occur in 2004 and 2012, with none at all taking place in the 20th century.) In 1716 Halley presented a paper to the Royal Society, calling for coordinated, worldwide preparations to begin at once.

So they began. The popular press covered the excitement. The best positions for observing Venus at the moment of transit were mapped out. Scientists from all over the world became involved. Several American scientists participated, including the surveyors Charles Mason and Jeremiah Dixon (surveyors of the Mason-Dixon line in the United States, which marked the boundary between North and South). Mason and Dixon would travel by ship to the Cape of Good Hope at the tip of Africa. In 1761 observers—122 of them—sighted the planet from 62 different locations, from Newfoundland and Siberia, from Peking and Calcutta, from Lisbon and Rome, from the Indian Ocean, and from St. Helena off Africa in the South Atlantic. It was perhaps the first great international scientific event, and the enthusiasm was intense, but despite the care with which the observations were made and the intense preparation, the results were not conclusive.

Because Venus is surrounded by a cloudy atmosphere, its edges are fuzzy in observation. As a result an effect known as the "Black Drop" or "Black Thread" kept even the most eager observer from being able to discern exactly when Venus had traversed completely into the disk of the Sun. Like a raindrop clinging to an umbrella, the outer edge of Venus seemed to cling to the surrounding sky. As a result measurements made even in the same location by key observers using identical telescopes turned out to be disappointingly different.

One more chance remained: the 1769 crossing. This time the number of sites was increased to 77 and the number of observers to 151, many in remote, isolated locations, including Baja California, the West Indies, Lapland, and the Arctic regions of Russia. Among the most famous was a singular voyage to the newly discovered island of

Captain James Cook exploring New Zealand aboard the *Endeavour*, 1769 (*Bettmann/CORBIS*)

Tahiti in the South Pacific, with the great scientist-explorer Captain James Cook at the helm of a hardy ship named the *Endeavour*.

It was the first of Cook's voyages in the Pacific, all of which gathered a wealth of knowledge about regions previously unknown to the European world. The primary purpose of the *Endeavour*'s expedition of 1768–71, of course, was the observation and measurement of the transit of Venus. Cook himself was an able astronomer, whose ability to navigate by the stars was prodigious. He was joined in the observation of Venus by astronomer Charles Green. In addition, the scientific team included Sir Joseph Banks, a wealthy young explorer-artist who provided the finances to purchase scientific supplies and equipment for the eight other members of the *Endeavour*'s international natural-history corps. Several prominent Scandinavian scientists were included, one of whom was a protégé of Carolus Linnaeus [lih-NAY-uhss], whose classification system of plants and animals, as we shall see in Part Two of this book, had, by 1753, already revolutionized the way people organized their thinking about living organisms.

The ship arrived in Tahiti in April 1769, allowing plenty of time to build an observatory (at a spot still known as Point Venus) before the moment of transit on June 3. But the day of the transit proved disappointing. As Cook wrote in his journal:

> Saturday 3rd. This day prov'd as favorable to our purpose as we could wish. Not a Clowd was to be seen the whole day and the Air was perfectly clear, so that we had every advantage we could desire in Observing the whole of the passage of Planet Venus over the Suns disk; we very distinctly saw an Atmosphere or dusky shade

round the body of the planet which very much disturbed the times of the Contacts particularly the two internal ones. Dr. Solander observed as well as Mr. Green and my self, and we differed from one another in observing the times of the Contacts more than could be expected. . . .

The conditions seemed perfect, but even so, the instruments were not powerful enough to provide definitive, accurate measurement.

Once all the measurements made of the transit of Venus world-wide in 1769 were compiled and analyzed—and it took nearly 60 years—the average value achieved turned out to be 96 million miles, actually much closer to the correct 93 million miles than any measurement made before. (The reading we accept today, achieved with an accuracy of several decimal places by radar measurement techniques, was not reached until the mid–20th century.) Based on the measurements made in 1769, the solar system had turned out to be nearly 100 times the size that Ptolemy had estimated the entire universe to be—a staggering change in worldview. But the scientists of the 18th century were not satisfied; they longed for more exacting measurement, and in this aspect of Cook's voyage, he was clearly disappointed.

Cook's other main objective in 1769 was to sail south to look for the great lost continent of Terra Australis Incognita. In this, too, he failed. But, as often happens in science, in his failure also lay his great achievement. For he sailed in waters never before explored. He discovered 70 islands he named the Society Islands, touched ashore in New Zealand, impaled his ship on the Barrier Reef, and discovered Botany Bay and Cook's Bay. His naturalists saw kangaroos for the first time, and Banks and his colleague, Daniel Solander, collected 17,000 new species of plants, as well as hundreds of species of fish and birds and skins of many animals. The artists aboard returned to Europe with drawings, sketches, and paintings of exotic places, native customs, and plants and animals the likes of which the people at home had never imagined. Of the other two voyages Cook would make to the Pacific, the last ended in tragedy, when he was killed by Hawaiians who only days before had worshipped him as a god. All three expeditions returned, however, with enormous discoveries about the peoples, flora, fauna, and landmasses of a world previously unexplored.

James Cook epitomized the kind of scientific eclecticism that prevailed in the 18th century, when a great navigator could contribute significantly to the science of astronomy with the precision of his measurements and observations; to geography with his maps and charts; and to botany, zoology, and anthropology with his copious observations and comparative descriptions. It was a time when great minds could contribute in many fields. In fact it was a time when those fields were not so clearly distinguished from each other as they would later become—a time when chemists were both physicists and physiologists, when geologists were also botanists and zoologists, and when mathematicians and musicians were also astronomers.

2

Stars, Galaxies, and Nebulas

FOR THOSE GAZING INTO DEEP SPACE and trying to unravel its mysteries, the 18th century had dawned with a brand-new set of challenges. Up until the end of the 17th century, the complex paths of the planets had absorbed most of the attention of positional astronomers. Records dating back thousands of years B.C.E. show that the earliest stargazers watched these "wanderers" and based complex philosophies and occult practices such as astrology on what they saw. The stars, by contrast, appeared to be more predictable, fixed in the skies, except for movements now explained by the revolution of the Earth around the Sun. The ancients—even the savvy ancient Greeks and the observant ancient Chinese—believed that the stars, unlike the planets, were unmoving. The great Greek philosopher Aristotle and, centuries later, his follower Ptolemy had envisioned a universe composed of nested spheres, layered like an onion around Earth, with the motionless stars embedded in the outer layer. The new 17th-century Copernican vision of the heavens straightened out a lot of the confusion about the solar system, recognizing the position of the Sun at the center. But even this new, revolutionary view of the universe placed the stars motionless beyond the edge of the planetary orbits. Copernicus, Kepler, and Newton, with his laws, had explained the motions of the planets. But if Newton's laws were truly "universal," then did the stars also have predictable movement? Newton did not address this question. For that we turn to a young disciple of Newton, Edmond Halley.

Of Stars and Comets

Edmond Halley was born in November 1656, the son of a wealthy London soap manufacturer. By the time he became a student at Oxford, he had developed an interest in astronomy, and at 19, while still a student, he published a work on Kepler's laws. The little book caught the attention of John Flamsteed, who became Britain's first Astronomer Royal that same year and had already begun putting together a new catalog of the stars in the Northern Hemisphere. Flamsteed, impressed with Halley's work, encouraged the young man to go further.

By the mid-1670s the improvement in telescopes and other instruments had revealed many inaccuracies in the old star charts and catalogs. New ones were badly needed. So, while Flamsteed and

The Remarkable John Goodricke

In the brief 21 years of his lifetime, astronomy offered John Goodricke both consolation and fame. Born in 1764 in the Netherlands, the son of an English diplomat, Goodricke spent his brief life in a world of silence, unable to hear or speak. His parents, though, were both wealthy and understanding and encouraged his interest in astronomy in his early teens. Under the night sky, sparkling with stars, Goodricke seemed to feel at home with his silence. Gifted with a keen mind and an observant eye, he turned each night to his telescope.

One star in particular caught his attention. Algol, in the constellation of Perseus, was a source of puzzlement for astronomers. Aristotle had taught that the stars were perfect and unchanging, but Algol, shining brightly in the sky, appeared to display a variability in its brightness. Perhaps it was this uniqueness that drew the young Goodricke to the star. Like him Algol was an anomaly, standing alone in its difference from the stars around it.

Goodricke took it upon himself to attempt to decipher the mystery of Algol, a job that called for excruciating patience and dedicated observation. Much of the work was done with the naked eye (that is, without the aid of a telescope), since he needed to make comparisons to stars beyond the field of vision of a telescope.

others were busy charting the northern skies, it occurred to Halley that the skies in the Southern Hemisphere were open territory to an ambitious astronomer. He convinced his father to finance his trip, and, taking leave from his studies at Oxford, Halley boarded a ship to chart the stars hanging over the Southern Hemisphere.

For the next year and a half, from 1676–78, Edmond Halley spent hour after lonely hour with little more than his telescope to keep him company on the bleak island of St. Helena, off the southwest coast of Africa. The weather was harsh and inhospitable, extremely bad for astronomical observation and no kinder to young Halley. But finally, his stay completed, Halley returned to England with a new and unprecedented catalog of the southern skies, listing the positions of no fewer than 341 previously uncharted stars. Halley had hoped to chart many more had the weather been more

Months of intense study and careful note taking convinced Goodricke that the star's variations followed a regular pattern, a specific period or cycle. After much more intense study, he was able to demonstrate that Algol went through its light changes in a regular period of just under three days. It was the first demonstrable proof of the regularity of a variable star.

In 1782 Goodricke attempted to answer the difficult question about the source of Algol's variation by suggesting that it was due either to dark spots on its surface or to a companion invisible to us that orbits the star, blocking the star's light from view at regular intervals. It was a daring hypothesis, especially when put forward by an unknown 17-year-old amateur astronomer. Goodricke's theory about Algol's mysterious orbiting companion would not be proved until much later—when it was discovered that Algol had not just one but two companions. However, though unproved, his paper won him the coveted Copley Medal from the Royal Society. Goodricke's death in 1786 came just before his 21st birthday, only two weeks after he was elected a fellow of the Royal Society. The young man had always suffered from ill health, and his death was attributed to overexposure to the cold night air.

Of the more than 36,000 variable stars known today, few are as easily explained as was the mystery of Algol, and Algol itself still contains many anomalies. Thanks to young Goodricke, though, another small chunk of knowledge was added to our understanding of the heavens.

favorable. But the work, published as *Catalogus Stellarum australium* (Catalog of the southern stars) in 1679, was enough to make Halley an immediate celebrity among London's scientific elite. Flamsteed heralded Halley as "the southern Tycho" (referring to the groundbreaking work of the great 16th-century Danish astronomer, Tycho Brahe). Years later Flamsteed would quarrel with Halley over the premature publication of one of Flamsteed's own star catalogs. But this was Halley's hour, and, gentlemanly and charming, he made the most of it. A tremendous success Halley was invited to join the prestigious Royal Society. It was heady company that young Halley suddenly found himself surrounded by, including such giants as Isaac Newton, Robert Hooke, John Flamsteed, and the charismatic Christopher Wren. But intelligent, modest, and personable, Halley found quick acceptance. Surprisingly he even struck up an immediate friendship with the reticent and usually sour-faced Newton. Among the first to see the *Principia*, Halley not only encouraged Newton to publish his revolutionary masterwork but paid for the publication out of his own pocket when the Royal Society's funds ran short. Money had never been a problem to Halley, and when his father was found mysteriously murdered, Halley's inheritance guaranteed him a comfortable income for life.

A life of leisure held little appeal for the intellectually curious Halley, however, and he was soon once again hard at work. During his long voyage south to St. Helena, he had observed that the ship's compass did not point exactly to the North Pole as was commonly believed. Thus the magnetic pole and the North Pole were not the same. Although the difference might be construed as minor, for navigators and ship's captains the discovery was an important one. The worldwide explosion of commercial trade during the latter part of the 17th century had opened up many new ocean routes, and competition was fierce. Just as new maps of the skies were needed, so too were new and better marine charts for use by seafarers for efficient navigation. In 1698, under the command of Halley, the first ship ever commissioned and outfitted solely for the purpose of scientific duties sailed out from London. Christened the *Paramour Pink*, the small but sturdy ship toured the seas for two years while Halley and his crew measured magnetic declinations around the world, composed new navigational charts, and attempted to determine the precise latitudes and longitudes for dozens of major ports.

Returning to London a seasoned sailor, Halley earnestly began another kind of research, this time delving through hundreds of stacks of ancient astronomy books and charts. During his journeys Halley had become intrigued with the many discrepancies between the ancient star charts and more contemporary ones. Despite the numerous outright and often outrageous errors in the old charts, he had noticed that many correctly charted stars still differed in their positions from modern observations. After careful study he was able to prove that at least three major stars, Sirius, Procyon, and Arcturus, had changed their position since the time when the Greeks had charted them.

What some astronomers were beginning to suspect, Halley proved to be true. The stars too were in motion. Even beyond the solar system, the objects of the universe appeared to be in constant dynamic and predictable movement—an idea inherent in Newton's laws of gravitation but unproved until Halley's careful work. Once again the ancient views of the universe were shattered under the power of Newton's grand gravitational and geometrical vision. This new piece of information would have enormous impact on astronomy in the years to follow.

Edmond Halley was the first to calculate the orbit of a comet, based on Newton's laws of motion. In this montage we see Halley's Comet and the European Space Agency (ESA) spacecraft *Giotto* that visited the comet during its 1986 appearance. *(Courtesy of ESA)*

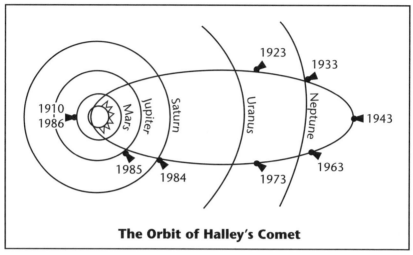

The Orbit of Halley's Comet

This diagram marks the progress of Halley's Comet along the length of its orbit since its last appearance in the nighttime skies.

But Halley is best known for his work with comets, long held in awe and superstitious reverence for their strange appearances in the night skies. As Halley pored over the ancient records, he discovered that he could see a pattern. When he attempted to calculate the shape of their orbits based on records of their appearances over the centuries, he saw that the calculations fit Newtonian theory. Precise information was sparse, however, and he was forced to abandon his project, but not until after he had made an interesting discovery. His calculations strongly suggested that four well-known comets, seen in 1456, 1531, 1607, and 1682, respectively, were in all likelihood just one comet, which, following Newton's gravitational laws, returned to the inner solar system on its orbit once every 76 years. It would return, Halley predicted, in 1758. Although he died in 1742, 16 years before he could see his prediction come true, the comet known today as Halley's Comet remains a dramatic tribute to the memory of the astronomer who first recognized the regularity of its movements.

New Views of the Universe

If the stars as well as the planets were in motion, then the universe beyond the solar system was no longer necessarily the sacrosanct, static, and perfect place it had always been thought to be. Also, if Newton's laws held true for all objects throughout the heavens, as observations had begun to indicate by the mid-18th century, then new perspectives and speculations about the universe in general were called for.

In the mid-1700s a handful of men put forward theories that began to revolutionize humankind's view of the cosmos and our own position in it. One of these was the French writer and naturalist Georges-Louis Leclerc, comte de Buffon, who will be discussed later in this book. Among the others were a deeply religious amateur scientist, a young speculator in philosophical ideas, and a brilliant mathematician.

THOMAS WRIGHT

Thomas Wright (1711–86) was an English thinker of many diverse interests. Well educated and well read in the prevailing philosophical and scientific views of his day, like many thinkers during the 1700s, he was troubled by the conflicts between his scientific observations and thinking and his religious beliefs. His astronomical observations and reading had led him to speculate that if the planets moving around the Sun formed an orbital system, then, given Newton's laws of gravity, it was possible that the stars themselves might also be a part of one or many similar orbital systems. If the heavens were thus composed, though, where was the domain of God in this new mechanistic and gravitationally interacting universe? Neither a trained astronomer nor a rigorous and systematic thinker, Wright actually proposed a number of different cosmological models. One of the earliest models pictured the Sun and solar system moving along with the stars to circle a huge common center, which might or might not be a solid, but nevertheless was the domain of God. On the outer region of this gigantic system, far beyond the solar system and stars, was a mysterious dark region of "doom" that surrounded all. It was a highly mystical concept, but further elaborations proved more fruitful. In his book, *An Original Theory and New Hypothesis of the Universe*, published in 1750, Wright suggested an alternative possibility: that rather than a shell-shaped universe in which the stars and solar system moved around a common center, the entire system might actually take the form of a flattened rotating disk. He still clung to the idea of a common center occupied by God or a divine presence, but he also suggested that the so-called nebulae, the mysterious murky white patches in the sky that were neither stars nor planets, lay far beyond the disk itself.

IMMANUEL KANT

A deeper and more rigorous thinker than Wright, the young German philosopher Immanuel Kant [KAHNT] (1724–1804) had either read Wright's provocative book or a review of it. In any event he quickly turned his razor-sharp mind to some of Wright's loosely formulated ideas.

In 1755 Kant offered his thoughts in his book *Allgemeine Naturgeschichte und Theorie des Himmels* (*Universal Natural History*

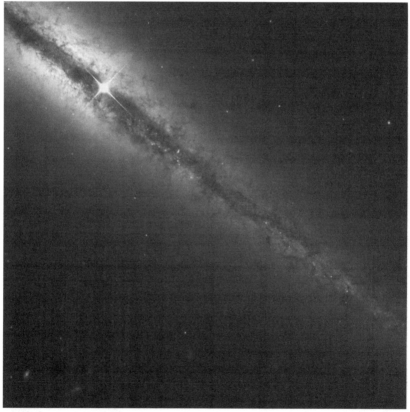

An edge-on view of the main disk of a distant galaxy (NGC 4013), as captured by the Hubble Space Telescope in 2001. Evidence shows that the dark band running the length of the disk's center is a region of interstellar dust where new stars may be forming. (*NASA*)

and Theory of the Heavens). As a work of speculative cosmology and astronomy, it was a truly remarkable achievement. Following Wright's lead and his own careful studies in Newton's physics, Kant suggested that the stellar system, like the solar system, was shaped like a flat disk. Just as the planets in the solar system revolve around the Sun in elliptical orbits in the plane of the zodiac, so, suggested Kant, the stars might also revolve around a common and unknown center.

Unlike Wright, Kant made no reference to a divinity occupying this hypothetical central position. Kant did suggest that the visible stars made up this common "galaxy," but that the system in which our Sun and planets participated in common revolution with other stars around an unknown center was probably not the only such system to exist in the universe. The universe, in fact, might be composed of many such galaxies. Kant further suggested that we may already have seen those other galaxies, that they might, in fact, be the nebulae observed by astronomers and mentioned by Wright. Many of these nebulae, Kant pointed out, were oval- or disk-shaped, and the combined light of the stars making them up might, at such a great distance away from us, create their milky and blurred appearance. It was an inspired and daring speculative leap, and, although not proved until the 20th century, it was one that opened up a vast new horizon for cosmology: an immense oceanlike universe filled with floating, rotating, island galaxies—a universe much larger and grander than anything any human could ever have dreamed.

It is important to remember here, though, that Kant's ideas, while based on his understanding of Newton's physics, were, however inspired, purely speculative. Although he was well read in physics and mathematics, Kant, who would later gain much fame and controversy as a philosopher, was neither a working physicist nor a mathematician.

Pierre-Simon Laplace

Not so Pierre-Simon Laplace, born in Normandy, France, in 1749. Laplace was a brilliant and inspired mathematician, one of the most influential scientists of the 18th century. Although he is largely unknown by most people today, his rigorous mathematical work nailed down some of the loose ends left by Newton and provided a stronger foundation for the speculation made by Kant.

Charles Messier and His Catalog

Charles Messier (1730–1817) was a comet hunter. Like many astronomers in his day and ours, he was fascinated with finding and tracking those elusive and dramatic visitors in the night skies. During his lifetime he was credited with discovering more than 15 new comets, earning him the nickname of Comet Ferret. Like most dedicated specialists, Messier was a little fanatic about his field of specialty and did not care to be disturbed with irrelevancies. Also, in the early days of his telescopic investigations, he found that he was constantly distracted by those small milky-white objects in the sky that were called nebulae (the Latin word for "clouds," which they resemble). Not much was known about them when Messier began his work. Immanuel Kant had made a few speculations, but William Herschel's classic work was yet to come, and anyway, Messier was after comets and could hardly care less about nebulae. His problem was simply that those nebulae could easily be mistaken for comets, moving very slowly in the distance, and a great deal of time could be wasted watching them to make sure that they were not comets but permanent fixtures in the night skies.

Messier decided that the only way to handle the problem once and for all was to compile a catalog, or list, of all the distracting nebulae and their exact positions in the sky so that other comet hunters would know exactly where they were located and would not waste valuable comet-hunting time on them.

It was a tough job, given the still primitive nature of the telescopes of his time and the task demanded a great deal of patience. Messier, however, was able to catalog 103 of these offending objects by 1781. Today many amateur as well as professional astronomers, wishing to view such wonders as the great Andromeda Galaxy (M31 in Messier's catalog—he preceded each entry with *M*, for *Messier*) and such other marvels as globular clusters, open clusters, planetary nebulae, and even a supernova remnant, can find them quickly thanks to Messier's famous work.

In 1773 Laplace made his first major contribution to astronomy when he examined the orbit of Jupiter in an attempt to understand why it appeared to be continuously shrinking while the orbit of Saturn appeared to be expanding. In a three-part paper published between 1784 and 1786, he demonstrated that the phenomenon was periodical—that is, occurred at regular intervals—and had a period of 929 years. While carefully explaining the reasons for the phenomenon, Laplace's paper also served to solve a major problem left open by Newton, that of the stability of the solar system. Newton, disturbed by the complex gravitational interactions among the bodies of the solar system, had concluded that some kind of divine intervention was needed occasionally to keep the entire system stable. Aided by fellow mathematician Joseph-Louis, comte de Lagrange (1736–1813), Laplace demonstrated mathematically that since all the planets orbit the Sun in the

Pierre-Simon, marquis de Laplace, succeeded in accounting for all planetary motion by applying Newton's theory of gravitation. Laplace's nebular hypothesis of stellar evolution offered a rational and fruitful approach to the question, How do stars form? *(The Royal Society, England)*

same direction, their eccentricities and inclinations in relation to one another always remained small enough to need no outside intervention to remain stable in the long term. Or, as Laplace wrote:

> From the sole consideration that the motions of the planets and satellites are performed in orbits nearly circular, in the same direction, and in planes which are inconsiderably inclined to each other, the system will oscillate about a mean state, from which it will deviate by very small quantities.

In effect, the solar system, said Laplace, was essentially a self-correcting mechanism, and it needed no divine force to nudge it back in place.

Laplace wrote many other important papers, shedding much mathematical light on several other large and small problems related

Joseph-Louis, comte de Lagrange, considered one of the greatest mathematicians of the 18th century, also worked on the motions of planets. *(Courtesy, Burndy Library)*

to Newton's theories and the gravitational interactions of the planets and satellites. His most popular and widely read work, however, came in 1796 when he published *Exposition du Système du Monde,* a popular work on astronomy, and in it, almost as an afterthought, offered a theory to explain the origin of the solar system.

The "nebular hypothesis," as Laplace's idea came to be called, had also been offered, perhaps unknown to Laplace, in a less rigorous and slightly differing form by Kant. Variously called the nebula hypothesis, Kant's nebular hypothesis, Laplace's nebular hypothesis, and the Kant–Laplace nebular hypothesis, the idea became immediately popular and was accepted by most astronomers throughout the 19th century.

In a much shortened form, and stripped of its mathematical framework, the idea was that in the beginning, the Sun originated as a giant rotating nebula or cloud of gas. As the nebula rotated and the gas contracted, the speed of its rotation increased until the outermost material in the nebula was moving too quickly to be held by its gravitational force. Stripped away, this gaseous material would then condense to form a planet, while the central nebula continued to increase its spin and contraction, eventually leaving behind more loosened material to form another planet, and so on, until all the planets were formed and the central nebula formed a stable Sun at the center. The theory was fraught with many problems and unanswered questions, but as an early attempt to explain the origin of the solar system using scientific and rational reasoning, without recourse to occult or metaphysical forces, it was an impressive beginning.

Laplace knew he had crossed over into speculation with much of his "theory," but he had no doubt that this and all other mysteries of the heavens would be resolved by the reasoned applications of mathematics and Newton's laws. Not the most modest of men nor the most gracious of scientists (he was often both hated and admired by his associates), he was one of the Enlightenment's most devout believers in the mechanistic nature of the universe. It was a belief held by many scientists during the Age of Reason, but few stated it as forcefully as Laplace, when he wrote that in Newton's universe, nothing happened by chance, and that in a hypothetical case, "an intelligence knowing, at a given instance of time, all forces acting in nature, as well as the momentary position of all things of which the universe consists, would be able to comprehend the motions of the largest bodies of the world . . . [and] nothing would be uncertain, both past and future would be present" in such a person's eyes.

Not all of Newton's followers during the 18th century were such ambitious philosophers, though. While theory still had its place, many astronomers, particularly in England, shied away from such grand theoretical speculations, preferring to take a more pragmatic and practical approach by employing the lessons of the Scientific Revolution and Newton's laws to everyday working astronomy.

Teamwork: William and Caroline Herschel

If the mathematician Laplace was the most influential theorist in astronomy during the 18th century, then the musician and amateur astronomer William Herschel [HUHR-shuhl] was the most influential working astronomer of the Enlightenment. Born in Hanover, Germany, in 1738, Herschel fled from military service in 1757 and moved to England. A renowned musician in Germany (oboist, organist, violinist, and concert master), he picked up his career in England, at first by teaching and copying music. In a short while, though, he was well established and began to find positions as a conductor of military bands and as a respected composer and organist. In 1766 he was hired to become organist at the Octagon Chapel in Bath. It was a good position, allowing him time to teach, conduct, and compose. More important to the history of science, the job paid well and supplied him with enough money to help finance his developing interest in astronomy. By the time his sister, Caroline (1750–1848), joined him in England in 1772, William had become so enamored of the stars and planets that he had devoured hundreds of books on astronomy, calculus, and optics. He had also purchased a small telescope and had begun to spend his nights gazing at the skies above Bath.

Caroline was quickly caught up in her brother's enthusiasms. An accomplished musician and singer, she was soon helping William with his orchestrations, copying his music, and displaying an almost equal fascination with astronomy and telescopes. It was only a short time after his sister's arrival when William, with Caroline's help, constructed his first small telescope. From that moment on there was no turning back. Another, slightly larger telescope followed quickly, and then another.

Interesting telescopes they were, moreover, much wider than the usual telescopes of similar length. When asked about their unusual structure, Herschel would explain that he was after not only magnification but also light-gathering ability. The larger the telescope's mirror, the more light it was capable of capturing, and the more light it captured, the more stars and nebulae he could see. Herschel had already become fascinated with the universe beyond the solar system. Over the long progress of his career, he would, with Caroline's help, define the discipline of stellar astronomy and focus the eyes of astronomers far beyond the mechanics of the solar system. Curiously, though, it would be a discovery within the solar system itself that would bring him his greatest fame, energize observational astronomy, and make him a worldwide celebrity.

Although Herschel could be a patient and precise observer (he once measured more than 100 different lunar craters, triple-checking himself by using three different methods), he was much more interested in discovery than in calculation. The night sky for Herschel was a vast, dark ocean, poorly charted and filled with the perpetual promise of new discoveries. To aid him in his nocturnal navigation through the heavens, he had devised a careful method of "sweeping" the skies. Each night he would work on only one small area of sky, usually a strip of only about two degrees, which he would explore twice before retiring. The next night he would examine an adjoining strip, gradually working around the entire night sky visible from his location.

During one of his careful sweeps in March of 1781, Herschel made his famous discovery of a new planet far beyond Saturn (the most distant planet known to astronomers at the time). Other astronomers had seen the planet, which soon was named Uranus, but everyone had always thought it was a star and quickly passed it by. During his nightly sweeps, though, Herschel had memorized the positions of thousands of stars, and he quickly recognized the small speck of light as a "wanderer," in a place where no star ought to be. Was it a comet or a planet? Reporting his discovery to the Astronomer Royal of the time, Herschel waited for his answer. A planet, reported the Astronomer Royal after calculating its orbit, definitely a planet, and so far away that it changed the size of the known solar system to nearly double what everyone had thought. William Herschel was suddenly famous.

William Herschel, who discovered the planet Uranus, was an accomplished musician who began his astronomical observations as an amateur. He soon became recognized as one of the greatest observational astronomers of the 18th century. (Courtesy, Burndy Library)

Curiously, after Newton, astronomy had become a pretty tame business in most everyone's eyes. Newton, after all, had explained everything, and just about everything that could be known was known. The theorists were working up their armchair philosophies, but most of them were pretty difficult to take seriously (if the average person ever heard about them at all), and the working astronomers were busy calculating and cataloging. New stars were occasionally announced, but for most people, a star was a star. A new planet, though—now that was something different, something unknown before and closer to home, something that the average person could actually imagine. And, even more exciting, maybe there were others yet to be discovered in the solar system. Maybe the scientists did not know everything there was to know after all.

This musician and amateur astronomer had suddenly made astronomy exciting again. The excitement was almost too much for Herschel, though. Appointed a fellow in the Royal Society, he was wined, dined, feted, and appointed court astronomer to King George III. This last honor had a major drawback, as Caroline quickly realized. With it went a pension, which was to enable her brother to quit his job as a musician and become a full-time

In 1772 Caroline Herschel arrived in England to join in her brother's observations. *(Stock Montage)*

astronomer. Unfortunately, the pension was considerably less than his earnings as a musician. As William pointed out, however, one did not turn down an appointment from a king. Other means would just have to be found to keep the money coming in. They were accomplished telescope builders, in fact, some had said their telescopes were the best in the world. The brother and sister would build and sell their fine instruments for additional income.

In the meantime, with more time on his hands to give to his new career, William could devote himself to building those wondrous, gigantic instruments he had always dreamed about, instruments that would enable him to look deep into space. "I have looked farther into space than ever [a] human being did before me," he wrote. Uranus had been a feather in his cap. In 1787 he also discovered Titania and Oberon, two of Uranus's moons, and, before he was finished, he added two more moons of Saturn. But Herschel's first love remained the starry realm—and the great telescopes that enabled him to peer into its depths.

Not all his telescopes were successes. One "monster" crashed under its own weight as Herschel was climbing to its mount. For another, planned around a mirror three feet in diameter, he had to use an "enormous amount of horse manure" (sifted and pulverized by the ever-enthusiastic Caroline) for the mirror's mold. The day of casting, the overheated mold cracked, sending molten metal cascading across the floor and turning the place into a miniature, foul-smelling Vesuvius, while Caroline and William took to their heels in frantic escape.

While it must have seemed to some people that the Herschels were spending all their time building telescopes, they managed to carve out more than enough time for their observations. And, when William married a wealthy woman in 1788, they were able to stop building telescopes for sale and concentrate on their own instruments and observing.

Edmond Halley had proved that the stars were not "fixed" but had "proper motion" in the skies. In 1783 Herschel made his first major "stellar discovery" when his observations proved that the Sun, too, was in motion across space. Our own solar system was moving in its entirety. The Sun, planets, and moons not only performed their intricate dance among themselves, but the dance floor itself was in motion as the entire system swept through the heavens. Not only was the Sun no longer the stationary center of the universe, but now, it appeared, neither was the solar system. Once more, humankind found that it held no privileged position in the universe, but inhabited a globe that was but one small participant in a great cosmic dance. More and more it became apparent to 18th-century thinkers that the entire universe was an endless dance of movement.

Not only was everything in motion, but there was more of "everything" than anyone could have imagined.

William Herschel had always been drawn to the mysterious patchy nebulae in the skies and to the conjectures by some thinkers that they were vast collections of stars too distant to be clearly seen. With his larger and more accurate telescopes, he was able to resolve many of them, proving once and for all that many were vast collections of stars, or galaxies. His early conclusion that all nebulae were vast galaxies of stars was later proved to be incorrect, as many nebulae refused to resolve into a clear demonstration of stars, but many of these were, he suspected, vast clouds of some "shining fluid" that was "the chaotic material of future suns."

Independent discoverer of eight comets, observational astronomer Caroline Herschel also collaborated closely in her brother's work. She lived to be 98 and dedicated her life to astronomy. *(Courtesy, Burndy Library)*

In a series of long observations of so-called double stars made with Caroline during the 1780s, he also proved that Newton's laws were indeed universal. His careful observations proved that many of the double stars were not just pairs but so relatively close to one another that they were locked by gravity into a mutual orbital dance. It was still further proof that Newton's laws stretch far beyond the solar system, throughout the entire vastness of space.

William Herschel was knighted in 1816, continuing his observations nearly up until the time of his death at the age of 83 in 1822. More than any other astronomer of the Enlightenment, Herschel brought astronomy into the modern age. His telescopic observations gave reality to the speculations of those thinkers during the Age of Reason who were beginning to see and understand humankind's place in the universe—that we on this humble planet called Earth were but one small part of a vast cosmos swimming with stars and galaxies.

For some this knowledge was frightening. Humankind and the Earth seemed to become more and more insignificant in the eyes of science, no longer the unique privileged and special creations of God. For others, though, a wonderful, new world of knowledge was opening up. As Halley, Herschel, and other observational astronomers began to show what *was*, thinkers like Kant, Laplace, and others attempted to understand *how*, given the apparently mechanistic nature of the universe, it all came to be. How did all the pieces fit together to form a whole? If the universe was filled with galaxies, by what process did the galaxies form? How did stars and planets form? How did the universe itself come to be? Did it have a beginning; did it have an end? They were big questions that would command many years even to develop into serious theories. Much more needed to be learned and many new instruments and techniques developed. Much more basic physics remained to be understood. What was this mysterious "gravity" that "controlled" so much? What was light? What was heat? How did the stars "shine"?

It was a demanding and complex agenda—one that would occupy many scientists for centuries. Not since the ancient Greeks had humans taken it upon themselves to attempt to explain so much. However, Newton had given them a key—and the thinkers of the Enlightenment believed they would readily be able to unlock all nature's mysteries with that key. That was both their glory and their hubris, for the task was far more complex than they ever imagined. Yet they made a noble effort and covered enormous ground.

3
Rocks and Ages
Birth of a New Geology

AS 18TH-CENTURY ASTRONOMERS continued to focus on the deep reaches of the cosmos and the fascinating realm of the solar system, another group of thinkers began to turn their attention to the history of the Earth itself—and its origin. If the heavens could be understood as a vast clockwork mechanism operating under Newtonian laws, was there also a mechanism that explained the creation of the diverse features of the Earth? Why were there lands and seas? Mountains and valleys? Different kinds of rocks? What were those strange features in some rocks that looked like embedded creatures or objects?

The ancient Greek philosophers had speculated on ways in which many of the Earth's features might have been formed. Thales [THAY-leez] of Miletus (ca. 624 B.C.E.–ca. 546 B.C.E.) had observed the violent power of waves breaking against the shore, and the less dramatic but no less persuasive power of the steady erosion of river beds by meandering rivers. It was quite obvious, said Thales, that water was tremendously important in its ability to change the features of the Earth. Water in fact was so important to Thales's thinking that he believed it to be the source of everything on Earth, both animate (living) and inanimate (nonliving). The Earth itself, said Thales, could be seen as a ship afloat in a gigantic ocean, and waves of disturbances in that ocean might be the causes of earthquakes as our planet bobbed in its surrounding environment. Although many of the ideas of Thales and the other ancient Greek thinkers may seem incredibly naive to us today, his recognition of the power of water as a fundamental force that helped to sculpt and form the surface of the Earth was an important early observation. His speculations, of course, were just that—speculations. The great Greek thinkers were philosophers, not scientists—and since the ancient Greeks had no desire and made no attempts to "prove" their ideas scientifically, there was no way that one speculation could be taken to be more correct than another. All comers had a right to an opinion, provided that their intellectual credentials were in order. As long as their ideas had internal consistency (that is, if all parts of their systems appeared to fit together without any one part contradicting another), then it was simply a matter of paying your money and taking your choice.

By the time the intellectual, commercial, and political power of the world shifted to Rome, in about 100 B.C.E., the Romans had abandoned most such speculations altogether. More practical than philosophic, the ancient Romans preferred to spend their time figuring out the best way to build roads, bridges, tunnels, and aqueducts to expand the power and prestige of the Roman world. For Romans it was a fruitless exercise to worry about how the mountains got there. Instead, their priorities called for figuring out the best way to build passable roads across or around them.

After the fall of Rome, when most intellectual activity in the Western world was confined to monasteries, much of the Western interest in learning shifted to the East. There, in the halls of learning of Islam, many of the ancient Greek and Roman ideas were preserved. Even the Arab intellectuals, though, who had borrowed, preserved, and expanded on much Greek learning, displayed little interest in what we today call geology. The great Islamic philosopher Avicenna (980–1037 C.E.) did attempt a rough-and-ready system, borrowing from and adding to some of the thoughts of the ancient Greeks, but there were still many problems with most of his explanations.

As the light of learning began to filter from the East slowly back into the Western world during the Renaissance (beginning mid–14th century), the study of geology remained low on the list of intellectual priorities. The brilliant artist Leonardo da Vinci, who took an interest in just about everything, put forth his ideas on the subject around 1508. Echoing some of Avicenna's thoughts, including the idea that mountains were created by the erosion of high lands, Leonardo also suggested that rivers were fed by rain and melting snow and that the intriguing and mysterious fossil shells that had been found in northern Italy were the remains of once living marine creatures that had died when the land was beneath saltwater. For the most part, though, Leonardo's thoughts on geology made little advance on Arab or ancient Greek thought.

The picture was further complicated by the presence of the Christian church, which almost single-handedly kept the flickering light of civilization alive through the Middle Ages, but had in the process grown into a powerful, single-minded, and authoritarian force. While the ancients had demonstrated only a passing interest in the problems of geology, they had not run into any formal or established opposition when they ventured into speculations on the subject. If they remained relatively silent or lacked profundity, their lack of progress was caused more by their own lack of interest or discipline than by interference by established authority.

With the increasing power of the Christian church, though, much had changed. In the 17th century Galileo had provoked the wrath of the church when his astronomical observations led him to the conclusion that the Sun and not the Earth was the center of the solar system. The idea was in direct conflict with established church doctrine based on the world of the Bible and the astronomical system handed down by Ptolemy. For the church the revealed word of God was sacred and the Bible was the final authority on all matters. Christians who might seek to understand the history of the Earth had merely to turn to the Bible for their answers. There in the stories of Genesis and the great catastrophe of Noah's flood was the history of the Earth encapsulated.

In 1654 an Irish prelate named James Ussher (1581–1656) had carefully calculated the age of the Earth according to biblical chronology. He had established Earth's first day as October 23 of the year 4004 B.C.E., probably at 9:00 A.M. He worked out the timetable for the entire creation of the universe as one week, as stated in the Bible. Ussher's calculations were well received at the time, since most theologians were agreed that the Earth could not be less than 5,000 or more than 6,000 years old. It was against this background that the early students of planet Earth and its formation began their work.

One of the problems, of course, as any careful observer could see, was that the Earth appeared much older than the few thousand years allotted for its existence. Everywhere one looked at its broken and weathered surface, its giant mountains, rugged cliffs and deep valleys, there was evidence of a planet that had suffered a great deal and gone through many changes. In fact, theologians generally agreed that the Earth was in serious decline and was probably not going to last much longer. How then had it changed so much in such a short period of time?

Another problem was the presence of fossils embedded inside rocks. Knowledge of fossils dated back to the ancient Greeks, but their existence had never ceased to be troubling. By the closing years of the 17th century, many serious thinkers had come to accept fossils as the organic remains of once living creatures. But, as we show later in this book, many others still held tightly to more mystical or Platonic views.

The two *F*'s, formations and fossils, intimately connected, were the prime focus of 17th- and 18th-century geological study.

Steno's Fossils

The first major thinker to examine these two major problems seriously was a 17th-century Dane who went by the name Niels Stensen (1638–86)—better known to us today as Nicolaus Steno. Born in Copenhagen, Steno was the son of a wealthy goldsmith. He trained in medicine, as so many early scientists did, and was fortunate enough to be appointed personal physician to the grand duke of Tuscany. With little to worry about, since the duke was both healthy and generous with his money, Steno had plenty of time to indulge his interests. One of those interests was fossils.

While dissecting sharks Steno compared their teeth with so-called tongue-stones, which the ancients believed fell from the heavens at night. After convincing himself that the tongue-stones were in reality petrified sharks' teeth, Steno became an avid collector of fossils, visiting rock quarries and examining different rock formations.

His careful studies convinced Steno of the truth of the ancient argument that the fossils were the remains of living creatures preserved in rocks that had once been laid down in the sea. In 1669 he published his arguments in a book with the unwieldy title *Prodrome to a Dissertation Concerning a Solid Naturally Enclosed Within a Solid.* Fossil-bearing rocks, Steno said, were created from the deposits of muddy water, both salt and fresh. Steno argued that some of the fossils, of sharks' teeth and seashells, for example, were obviously marine, and so salty seas must once have covered all the inland places in which Steno found them. Others, he pointed out, represented creatures that had lived in freshwater and had probably been carried to their destinations by Noah's flood, which was generally believed to have occurred around 4,000 years before Steno's time. The big bones and teeth that were found were most likely the remains of much more recent creatures such as the elephants that had moved Hannibal's army against Rome in 218 B.C.E.

He also suggested a reasoned method by which gigantic layers of rocks formed from underwater deposits might collapse and create mountains and valleys. Not all the mountains were created in this way, though, according to Steno. Some were obviously volcanic, vomiting out ashes and rocks from fires burning deep within the Earth, and still others had been etched out by running waters in the same process by which cliffs and gorges were cut by running streams.

Steno also offered some general theories on the geological history of Tuscany, which, he speculated, might also be applicable to the entire Earth. All in all it was an impressive, if faulty, performance, but Steno, an extremely religious Lutheran, failed to follow it up. Always a deeply troubled man, he apparently underwent some kind of dramatic spiritual crisis. Losing interest in geology altogether, he converted to Catholicism and spent his last days living in harsh and continual penance as a priest in Germany.

It is difficult to appreciate Steno's heroic intellectual effort outside the framework of his time. A few others, such as that ubiquitous English fellow of the Royal Society Robert Hooke, were attempting similar rational theories. But most late 17th-century speculations about the creation of the Earth and its formation, some of which carried well over into the 18th century, either remained deeply religious or were awkward attempts to bind together the religious version of the story with the new scientific views. One, however, that stands out is the theory put forth by Georges-Louis Leclerc, comte de Buffon (1707–88), whose extensive work in the life sciences we'll come back to in Part Two of this book.

Buffon Tests the Earth

A naturalist at heart, Buffon felt his vast work *Histoire naturelle* (*Natural History*), published in 44 volumes beginning in 1749, should begin at the beginning. "The general history of the Earth," he wrote, "must precede the history of what it has produced." Most of his ideas

Georges-Louis Leclerc, comte de Buffon, had a brilliant and wide-ranging career in science. He wrote a 36-volume work on natural history, and his naturalistic account of the origins of the Earth was one of the first of his time not closely tied to the biblical account. Here he is using multiple lenses to test the claim that Archimedes could have set fire to the Roman fleet in the harbor of Syracuse by focusing the Sun's rays on the ships. Based on his own success at setting fire to objects 150–250 feet away, Buffon concluded the story could be factual. *(Figuier,* Vies des savants, *1870)*

were just a restatement of prevailing ideas of the time. But his discussion of the shaping of the Earth created a shock for the conservative minds of his French contemporaries.

"In effect," he wrote, "it appears certain that the Earth, now dry and inhabited, was formerly under the waters of the sea. These waters were above the summits of the highest mountains, since we find on these mountains and even on their peaks the remains of sea life and of shells which, compared to shells now living, are the same. We cannot doubt their perfect resemblance or identity of their species." Many of Buffon's ideas were (as we know today) incorrect—and many others were neither new nor original. But, fitted together into a comprehensive (if very general) whole, they were tremendously stimulating to those 18th-century thinkers who, like Buffon, were trying to give new and rational answers to the old questions about the universe.

Borrowing an idea from the philosopher Leibniz, the Earth, Buffon said, was created when a comet collided with the molten Sun and knocked a piece from it. He ran some experiments with iron balls, which he heated, measuring the rate at which they cooled. From these results he estimated the rate at which a similar ball the size of the Earth would have taken to cool. Thus, based on the experimental cooling time needed, he concluded that the Earth was also very old. Perhaps, he suggested, as old as 75,000 or 100,000 years. Of course recent evidence points to an age closer to 4.6 billion years, but Buffon's estimate was much older—more than 10 times more—than the 6,000 years calculated by James Ussher in 1654. James Hutton, who will be discussed later in this chapter, would reach a similar conclusion about the Earth's great age years later (he, too, would greatly underestimate it, though). But Buffon was the first to reach a wide audience with the idea. Always politically astute, Buffon avoided major conflicts with the church over his ideas by offering his work only as hypotheses and managing to maintain a religious link in his chain of events.

The Earth, according to Buffon's hypothesis, had gone through a period of seven long epochs. This coincided nicely with the seven days of creation as taught in the Bible—but the "days" were a lot longer than literal days as we know them. After the initial epoch—formation of Earth caused by the collision of a comet with the Sun—the Earth rotated and cooled for around 3,000 years while it evolved into a spheroid. The second epoch found Earth congealing and hardening into a solid body. This, according to Buffon's calculations, probably took around 30,000 years. During the third epoch the vapors from the gases surrounding the Earth formed a gigantic universal ocean that covered the planet. During this period, he explained, tidal action began to shape the Earth's development and distributed sea creatures (the origin of fossils) all over the Earth. He calculated that this process lasted nearly 25,000 years. Volcanic activity dominated the fourth epoch as the ocean began to subside over the next 10,000 years, leaving the remains of many marine creatures on high, dry land. As land began to surface and cool, vegetation began to grow. Then, during the fifth epoch, lasting some 5,000 years, the first land animals began to appear. During the sixth epoch the land continued to evolve as vast continents began to separate from each other, drifting for nearly 5,000 years until they arrived at their present formation. Finally, at last, in the seventh epoch, proclaimed Buffon, humans appeared on Earth to reap the harvest of all that had gone before.

It was an audacious, neat, and compact bit of speculative theory, and it offered vast appeal—especially since it was able to explain many mysteries, such as marine fossils discovered on high land and mountain tops.

Buffon tended to sidestep most scientific-religious conflicts throughout his work, though, and real progress was not made in geology until the full-scale onslaught on tradition by the Enlightenment thinkers freed scientists to follow the indications they found in the rocks and the formations they observed.

As more researchers began to explore the field, it quickly became apparent to investigators that certain kinds of rocks, those termed *sedimentary*, had been laid down in parallel layers, or strata, and were formed from materials deposited underwater. The presence of fossil sea creatures embedded in those rocks helped to confirm this idea, but a disturbing problem remained. Many stratified rocks had been discovered in even the highest and most mountainous regions. Clearly, vast areas of what was now dry land must once have been under the sea, and it was during that time that the material that currently made up stratified rocks was deposited. How then had the land emerged from the sea after the rocks were formed? Like many other blossoming scientific fields in the post-Newtonian era of the Enlightenment, the early days of geology were dominated by the search for mechanisms.

Two opposing theories quickly became preeminent, and both eventually fell out of favor. Yet each contributed in its own way to the pioneering work of Charles Lyell (1797–1875), the persevering Scottish geologist who would lay the foundations for modern geology in the following century. He would also give both geologists and biologists a new key to understanding the Earth and human history upon its surface.

Abraham Werner and Neptune's Leavings

Abraham Gottlob Werner, the most famous geologist of his time, was born in Prussia in 1750. His father was an inspector in a large ironworks, and Werner spent most of his youth fulfilling his own interest in mines and minerals. After spending two years (1769–71) at the Mining Academy at Freiberg, he moved on to the University of Leipzig to continue his studies. A brilliant student, he pursued his studies avidly, absorbing everything he could get his hands on about mines, minerals, rocks, and mineralogy.

In 1775 Werner returned to the Freiberg Academy to become a lecturer. He would stay at Freiberg for nearly 40 years, becoming in his time not only the most famous but also the most popular instructor at the school. A dynamic and hard-driving "hands-on" teacher, Werner encouraged his students to travel the countryside and study rocks and mines for themselves rather than rely exclusively on the opinions of others. That was the idea, anyway. Unfortunately he was somewhat dogmatic about his own views and most of his students' fieldwork was heavily indoctrinated by his ideas.

What Werner taught was a theory of the Earth that came to be known as Neptunism. The name (derived from the Roman god of the sea) reflects Werner's first basic premise: that the Earth was originally covered entirely by a vast, muddy primeval ocean. Suspended within this ocean were huge quantities of materials that, as the sea level began to decline, crystallized onto the seabed as "primary" rocks. Those rocks, explained Werner, were the universal formation that became the whole original surface of the Earth. Werner didn't attempt to explain where the original ocean came from, or by what mechanism it began to recede. The ocean's recession continued, though, according to Werner, and much later the first dry land (the original deposition of rocks) was exposed.

Gradually new layers of rocks, which could no longer be considered a part of the original formation, were laid down as further material crystallized from the ocean, as well as from sediments eroded away from the original Earth's surface. With the ocean retreating still further, greater areas of land became exposed, including not only these "tran-

Geologist Abraham Gottlob Werner developed the theory of Neptunism, stating that a vast ocean covered the Earth during its formation and all rocks therefore formed through sedimentary processes. *(Courtesy, Burndy Library)*

sition" rocks, but also great mountains formed by the original (primary) rocks laid down many years before.

Then, continued Werner, massive erosion of the surface swept huge amounts of sediment back into the ocean, where it deposited and formed the strata of "secondary" rocks. Violent storms and temporary changes in the sea level caused irregularities in the depositions of the secondary rocks. Then, as the sea began to decline again, these layers of secondary rock were also exposed to further erosion and deposition into the sea, becoming new alluvial formations. Only recently, explained Werner, had the sea receded still further, allowing us to see these rocks that can be found only in the most low-lying areas.

Volcanoes, which seemed to trouble some of his contemporaries so much (some thought that all land might be volcanic in origin), were of little importance in the formation of the Earth's crust, according to Werner. He explained that they were probably caused by seams of coal burning near the Earth's surface.

Among those troubled by volcanoes (but not buying into the idea that all land was volcanic in origin) was James Hutton, Werner's contemporary and senior. Although he did not put forward his own ideas on the formation of the Earth's surface until 1788, Hutton's views, which came to be known as Plutonism, formed the greatest geological debate in the second half of the 18th century.

James Hutton and Pluto's Belchings

Born in Edinburgh in 1726, James Hutton was a pragmatic Scotsman who, after completing an apprenticeship in law, took a degree in medicine from the University of Leiden in 1749. He never practiced but turned to agriculture instead. Then, after a short stint as a farmer, he turned manufacturer, making a great deal of money from a factory he founded for the manufacture of ammonium chloride, after which he retired to study geology. It was not as much a round-the-barn trip as it appeared. His early interest in chemistry had led him into medicine, and this interest also flowed into mineralogy as he began to study the rocks and soil of his farm.

Hutton's new and, for the time, controversial theory was first published in the *Transactions* of the Royal Society of Edinburgh in 1788, although he had been working on it for more than 20 years. Hutton did not argue with Werner's observations that the sedimentary rocks had been laid down underwater, but he did dispute the claim that all the material forming those rocks had once been suspended in a vast primeval ocean that covered the entire Earth.

In Hutton's theory, based on systematic observations and thinking, he not only proposed an alternative to the Neptunists but also laid down an important principle, for which he is often named the founder of geology. That principle, known as Actualism, proposes that the Earth's surface was formed by forces—erosion and volcanoes—that were still active in modern times and could still be observed. It is closely linked with a principle known as Uniformitarianism, further developed in the following century by Lyell, which combines Actualism with several other factors to form many of the basic premises on which modern geology is based.

Werner had refused to speculate about the origin of the Earth and the primeval ocean (although many others, including Buffon, were doing that). His theory simply assumed the primeval ocean had existed and that conditions had once been very different from those operating today.

Hutton assumed (perhaps based on his religious beliefs) that both land and sea came into existence nearly simultaneously, proposing that we could only understand what the evidence presented to us about the Earth's "continuing" process and see it as an indefinite cycle with "no vestige of a beginning—no prospect of an end."

The land's surface, he explained, is slowly eroded by wind, water, and frost. The debris is then carried out to sea by rivers, where it is deposited on the bottom.

At the bottom of the sea, pressure and heat from deep within the Earth then "bake" the strata into sedimentary rock. Different layers of rock could be formed depending on the nature of the land erosion. Later, upward pressure on the seabed raises it through a series of earthquakes until the sedimentary rock is exposed as dry land. Much of this rock, Hutton continued, could have been deformed in the long, slow process, and cracks in it might have allowed molten rock from deep within the Earth to seep upward, where, upon reaching the surface, it might form volcanoes. Igneous rock, formed by heat, might also work its way into the strata of sedimentary rock. There it would slowly cool and form crystalline rocks such as granite. Meanwhile the steady process of erosion is continuing and is already beginning to wear away the new land surface. While further erosion wears down some of the sedimentary rock and exposes the

Volcanic eruptions in Europe in the 18th century focused attention of many geologists on Earth's internal heat and its role in the formation of the planet's crust. (*Figuier,* Vies des savants, *1870*)

granite, new layers of sedimentary rock continue to form on the seabed. This rock, too, may then be forced upward by pressure and movements within the Earth, continuing the cyclical process, a process that continues today.

Hutton saw that this process was not only machinelike, but he recognized that changes observed in the present could account over a long period of time for observed features of the Earth's crust—the principle that became known as Actualism. Hutton proposed that these long cycles had been operating in the same slow way and at the same slow rate, throughout the Earth's history. He also saw that the Earth's history must be very long—much longer than most scientists had suspected—and that the Earth was therefore much more ancient than anyone believed.

In 1795 Hutton expanded and published his theory in a two-volume book entitled *Theory of the Earth*. The few people who found it readable (he was a terrible writer) also found it controversial. Werner's followers took it as a direct attack on Werner's Neptunian system, and conservative theologians saw it as an attack on the account of creation as related in the Bible. Still, Hutton's Plutonism (named after the god of the underworld, since much of the energy required for Hutton's cyclical changes came from the internal heat of the Earth) picked up some devoted followers. A few more disciples were added in 1802, when John Playfair straightened out much of Hutton's unwieldy prose and offered Hutton's theories in a much more accessible form in his book *Illustrations of the Huttonian Theory*.

It would be nice to be able to report that Hutton was right and his theory won the day. Neither history nor science is quite that simple, though. While Hutton's basic premise—that the geological changes in the Earth were uniform and cyclical, and operated over a long period of time—was essentially correct, his explanation of the mechanism of change was wrong. In the 19th century Charles Lyell would pick up Hutton's Uniformitarian principles and put the pieces together to give the world a truer picture.

Georges Cuvier and Catastrophism

The Neptunism vs. Plutonism debate dominated geology for most of the latter part of the 18th century—and matters were not helped by the intrusion of the famous French zoologist Georges Cuvier into the picture. Cuvier (1769–1832), whose contributions to the life sciences will be discussed further later in this book, was one of the most powerful scientists of his time. Brilliant, opportunistic, and convinced of the correctness of his own opinions, Cuvier had studied fossils extensively and arrived at the conclusion that their existence could only be explained if the world had been subject to a series of major floods throughout its history. Each of these many floods, Cuvier argued, destroyed all living things on Earth, leaving behind only a fossil record. After each flood, life was created anew. The view had appeal to a great many religious thinkers, especially since Cuvier explained that the last great catastrophe (his theory was later called Catastrophism) was the flood described in Genesis, the first book of the Bible. During that catastrophe, Cuvier explained, God had intervened, permitting some living things to survive, as the Bible described in the story of Noah. Obviously Cuvier decreed, and many listened, the Earth did not undergo a continuing process of slow and gradual change as Hutton had argued, but was instead the product of a series of violent calamities.

Cuvier was so powerful that his dramatic theory of Catastrophism soon superseded the less exciting "primeval ocean" mechanics of Werner and all but knocked Hutton and his Plutonism out of the picture. Both Werner and Hutton were specialists, not generalists, and both had attempted to treat geology as a science. Both had proposed mechanisms that they each believed fitted the facts as they observed them (although Hutton is sometimes accused of being too casual in his fieldwork). Both were pursuing avenues that proved unproductive, even though Hutton's Actualism opened up a direction that would prove fruitful in the future. But Cuvier's prodigious reputation as a careful methodologist and seasoned theorist captured the imaginations of most scientists at the time. And his giant shadow discouraged healthy questioning in geology for the rest of the 18th century and well into the 19th century.

4
The Birth of Modern Chemistry

ON MAY 8, 1794, AT THE PEAK of the Reign of Terror in France, Antoine-Laurent Lavoisier, one of the greatest scientists of all time, was hauled away to his fate at the guillotine. As one of the old, deposed royal-government tax collectors, he was seen by many as a public enemy, a member of the Fermiers Généraux, who made a profit by skimming a fee off the top of taxes paid to an unpopular king by a poor and downtrodden populace. On top of that offense, Lavoisier (1743–94) had opposed the admission of Jean-Paul Marat (a journalist who fancied himself a scientist) to the French Academy of Sciences, a move that turned out to be disastrous because Marat never forgot the blackball. When Marat gained power in the revolutionary government in France, he saw a way to gain revenge and had Lavoisier arrested, tried, and convicted. A key force in the Reign of Terror that washed the streets of Paris in blood, Marat was himself arrested and guillotined before Lavoisier. But the wheels of bureaucracy were not reversed; the Revolutionary Tribunal had passed its sentence, announcing, "The Republic has no use for scientists." Lavoisier's sentence was carried out as scheduled.

It was a grim day in the history of science, for Lavoisier—with the help of four other great chemists, Carl Wilhelm Scheele, Joseph Priestley, Joseph Black, and Henry Cavendish—had finally, just a few years before, begun to unravel the chaos that had reigned in chemistry since ancient times. Lavoisier had brought the Scientific Revolution to chemistry just five years earlier with his *Traité Elémentaire de chimie* (*Elementary Treatise on Chemistry*) published in 1789. At 51 he was at the height of his potential. In the words of Joseph Louis

Antoine-Laurent Lavoisier and the Fermiers Généraux stand trial before the Revolutionary Tribunal. Though recognized by his contemporaries as a great scientist, Lavoisier was sentenced to be guillotined. *(Figuier,* Vies des savants, *1870)*

Lagrange, spoken on the day after Lavoisier's execution, "It took but a moment to cut off that head; perhaps a hundred years will be required to produce another like it."

Cooks and Mystics

Scottish chemist Joseph Black liked to tell his audiences, "Chemistry like all other sciences, had arisen from the reflections of ingenious men on the general facts which occur in the practice of the various arts of common life." Chemistry—partly because it was so much involved with the everyday stuff of life—was, of all the scientific disciplines, the slowest to emerge from the Middle Ages, to throw off the old confused approaches and enter the post-Newtonian age. The free development of chemistry was, on the one hand, victim of the stigma of being too common and everyday (Greek philosophers, in particular, disdained any discipline that involve using one's hands and chemistry was closely identified with cooking, the trades, and medicine). On the other hand it was stymied by its classification as a secret in the hands of alchemists who sought to transmute, or change, other substances into gold. (Some alchemists kept mum because they were naive enough to believe that they were close to a breakthrough; the rest sought silence because they did not want to get caught in their hoax.) Chemistry, of all the sciences, resisted application of the scientific method in the hands of early experimenters. Physics had the universal laws of motion discovered by Newton; astronomy had the discovery of the rotation of the Earth and its revolution around the Sun; biology had William Harvey's work on the movement of blood and the action of the heart. But chemistry had resisted any such breakthrough, understandably, given more recent 20th-century theories about the formation of compounds and the complex processes that take place at the molecular level in chemical reactions. All this was completely unknown in the 18th century; atomic theory as we know it had not yet even been conceived of.

As a result, at the beginning of the 18th century, great confusion reigned among those whose interests concerned the mixture and heating of substances. Scientists had no hope of ever making any progress until they had a handle on basic facts about air and water, the existence of "gases," and the process of combustion. It proved one of the most stubborn series of problems facing scientists in the 18th century, revolving around such basic issues that today seem mystifying to us as questions at all—until we put ourselves in the shoes of 18th-century thinkers. The processes of combustion, calcination (the process that takes place when a substance is heated to a high temperature, but below the fusing or melting point), and respiration were recognized as crucial and interrelated, but exactly how was elusive. Many fine minds expended a great deal of time on this problem, from the time of Robert Boyle and Robert Hooke and to the end of the 18th century.

Birth of the Phlogiston Theory

Unfortunately the first effort at establishing an integrated theory to explain combustion took science down one of those long side roads that lead virtually nowhere. The idea came, originally, from a man named Johann Joachim Becher [BEK-uhr] (1635–82), a latter-day alchemist who sold some city leaders in Holland on the claim that he could use silver to turn tons of sand into great heaps of gold. When his demonstrations did not work, he fled to England. His ideas about matter were not much sounder. All bodies, he said, consisted of air, water, and three kinds of earth, which he called *terra pinguis* (fatty earth), *terra mercurialis* (mercurial earth), and *terra lapida* (stony earth).

In the late 17th century, Georg Ernst Stahl (SHTAHL) (1660–1734) changed the name of Becher's *terra pinguis* to *phlogiston* [floh-JIS-tahn], which he described as a potent—"fire, flaming, fervid, hot"—fluid that was released or lost by any substance when it burned, calcinated, or otherwise oxidized (though that term was not yet used). In 1697 Stahl set forth his doctrine of phlogiston, and it became the framework that served to explain a constellation of puzzling chemical phenomena, the be-all and end-all of chemistry for more than 90 years.

Even though phlogiston did turn out to be a blind alley, not all consequences were negative, since it stimulated endless experiments on combustion, oxidation, respiration, and photosynthesis.

These experiments soon revealed glaring problems, though. For one thing a metal's oxide always weighed more, not less, than the original metal. If a substance was lost in a process, weight would normally be lost, not gained. To explain this without tossing out the theory, many chemists put forth ever more complicated explanations: Perhaps, since one could not really see phlogiston (only the flame is evidence of its exit from the burning substance), it was not a normal substance. Maybe it was more like one of the phenomena that 18th-century chemists assumed to be "subtle" or "imponderable fluids," such as magnetism, ether, heat, light, and electricity, and, like them, had no weight. Maybe, even, it had negative weight, so that when it was present in the substance, it actually (somehow) *subtracted* weight from it. So when combustion took place, phlogiston was released and the weight of the substance increased.

But, despite this nagging weight problem, most chemists of the 18th century continued to subscribe to the phlogiston theory, seeing no compelling reason to abandon it, and, nonetheless, made landmark contributions to the study of gases in particular.

Gases, chemists had begun to find, had the greatest potential for responding to scientific inquiry about chemical makeup. Breakthroughs in this area laid groundwork for discoveries about other elements and compounds and, ultimately, in the 19th century, atomic theory. Stephen Hales, a parish priest and amateur scientist in England, made these breakthroughs possible by his invention of a device for collecting gases, the pneumatic trough. The device separated the flask in which a reaction took place from the vessel in which he collected the gas, and in this way was able to separate different gases. But he, like most chemists at the time, did not really recognize that these were essentially different substances. He just thought they were different types of air.

Joseph Black and "Fixed Air"

To physician-chemist Joseph Black (1728–99), professor of chemistry at the University of Glasgow and, later, the University of Edinburgh, would go the honor not only of discovering carbon dioxide but also of establishing quantitative analysis.

Born in Bordeaux the son of a Scots-Irish wine merchant, Black went back to the British Isles in 1740 for his education. After completing his studies in medicine at the universities of Glasgow and Edinburgh, he returned to Glasgow to practice and teach. Highly respected by his students (of whom James Watt was one, as well as a friend), he was described by one of them as a man who "possessed that happy union of strong but disciplined imagination, powers of close undivided attention, and ample sources of reasoning, which forms original genius in scientific pursuits."

In his later years, wrote his student, "his countenance continued to preserve that pleasing expression of inward satisfaction, . . . easy, unaffected, and graceful."

As a young man working on his thesis, Black was investigating a major component in "Mrs. Joanna Stephens's secret remedy" for treating bladder stones (for which she sold the recipe to Prime Minister Robert Walpole for £5,000) when he discovered "fixed air." The component was calcined snails, which Black proceeded to test, using the quantitative methods he had developed. Many of the terms used in his descriptions of his experiments are unfamiliar today—quicklime, calx, and so on—because his work preceded Lavoisier's highly useful reorganization of chemical nomenclature. But, in modern terms, he found that calcium carbonate converted to calcium oxide when heated strongly, giving off a gas that could then recombine with the calcium oxide to re-form calcium carbonate. Because the gas could be recombined, or fixed, back into the solid it came from, he called it "fixed air." Today we are more familiar with it as carbon dioxide.

Others actually had done some previous work with carbon dioxide, but Black was much more thorough. He showed that carbon dioxide could be obtained by eating, by decomposition of a mineral, as well as by combustion and fermentation. He also made a breakthrough with regard to gases, demonstrating that they could be manipulated and tested in much the same way liquids and solids could be tested. Black recognized that carbon dioxide was a natural component of the air, that people breathe out carbon dioxide, and that a candle could not burn in it. Here he came upon a puzzling point. A candle placed in air in a closed container would finally go out. This was logical, since a burning candle produced carbon dioxide. But when Black used chemicals to absorb the carbon dioxide, the candle still would not burn in the closed container. He gave the problem to one of his students, Daniel Rutherford, who wrote his doctor's thesis on it.

Rutherford performed carefully controlled experiments and found that not only did a candle not burn in this gas, but a mouse could not live in it either. Like his teacher he was a subscriber to the phlogiston theory, and he believed that this air had taken on all the phlogiston it could contain (so phlogiston could not pass out of the air to the candle to burn or to the mouse for respiration). He called it "phlogisticated air"; today we call it nitrogen. Rutherford usually receives the credit for the discovery of this noxious gas, although the details were not clarified until a few years later by Lavoisier.

Black's quantitative approach, which he passed on to his students and the scientific world at large, proved as important as his discovery of carbon dioxide. As he applied heat to the calcium carbonate in his original experiment, Black took measurements of the loss of weight involved. This gave him clues about what was taking place in the reactions—clues that chemists had not had before in their dealings with gases.

Once he had discovered fixed air, Black wrote, "a new and perhaps boundless field seemed to open before me. We know not how many different airs may be thus contained in our atmosphere, nor what may be their separate properties." In this he seemed to point forward to the coming discoveries of Cavendish and Priestley in his own time and of others, such as Baron Rayleigh and Sir William Ramsay, who would receive the Nobel Prize for their work on the constituents of the atmosphere in 1904. Black's work in the field of physics, which will be discussed in the next chapter, was equally important, with far-reaching consequences for the Industrial Revolution.

Henry Cavendish Analyzes Water

Henry Cavendish (1731–1810) was without question the most eccentric scientist in the 18th century. Born to a famous and wealthy British family, he never had to worry about money. In fact he once told his banker that if the banker ever bothered Cavendish about what to do with his money, the bank would lose his account, which was worth millions. Needless to say, the banker never bothered him again. But where other Cavendishes had hobnobbed with kings and participated in grand political plots, Henry's one and only interest was the pursuit of pure science.

Cavendish was a recluse to the extreme. He did not like to see people and he did not like to talk to people. (The portrait in this book, based on a painting by W. Alexander in the British Museum, is probably the only one in existence.) One day, after catching sight of a maid by chance in his house, he had an extra stairway built—one for his use alone, so that the incident would never happen again. The maid, according to one account, was fired. Unfortunately Cavendish also published only selected bits of his work and consequently did not get credit (and the scientific community did not get the benefit) for several achievements that he was the first to make.

Some of his work did become known to his contemporaries, though. In 1766 he

Personally eccentric, Henry Cavendish discovered hydrogen, explored the properties of carbon dioxide (called "fixed air" in his time), and showed that water is not an element, contrary to Aristotle's pronouncements. *(Edgar Fahs Smith Collection–University of Pennsylvania Library)*

presented a paper to the Royal Society on "Factitious Air," which demonstrated the existence of a distinct flammable substance not previously studied (later named *hydrogen* by Lavoisier). He also studied the properties of carbon dioxide, which he, like Black, called "fixed air."

And his most signal achievement he did publish. On January 15, 1784, he demonstrated that his Factitious Air, when burned, produced water. This was a stunning bit of news. Aristotle had maintained that water was one of the four indivisible elements of which all substances were made. But if water was formed from burning a gas, then the only explanation had to be that it was formed from the combination of two gases. It was the death knell for the Greek system of elements.

Cavendish, like Black, did extensive work in physics, which will be covered in the next chapter, but he also experimented with air, passing electric sparks through it in 1785. To explain what he did in modern terms, he forced the nitrogen in the air to combine with oxygen, then dissolved the oxide he obtained in water. (In the process he figured out how to produce nitric acid.) He kept adding more oxygen, with the expectation that eventually he would use up all the nitrogen. But a small amount of gas—just a bubble—remained behind. Now, speculating a bit, he figured that this small amount of gas must be something not encountered before, very resistant to chemical reaction, in fact, what we would call inert. Henry Cavendish had discovered argon, although it would not be verified until a century later, when William Ramsay followed up.

Scheele and Priestley Discover Oxygen

Joseph Priestley (1733–1804) was an English Unitarian minister and a radical in politics, which eventually created problems for him later in life. He openly supported the American colonists in 1776 in their revolt against George III. He opposed slave trade and religious bigotry. He also sympathized with the French Revolution. Most of his 150 books, one of which was publicly burned in 1785, were religious and educational. Moreover, his introduction to the study of gases may seem unusual: He began his experiments at a local brewery in the town of Leeds, where he lived—and he discovered that Joseph Black's fixed air produced a pleasant, bubbly drink when mixed with water, producing carbonated water. In essence Priestly had invented soda water.

Growth of Scientific Societies

Scientific societies came in many shapes and sizes during the science-conscious 18th century. Small, informal groups like the Lunar Society, founded around 1766 by Matthew Boulton, were frequently formed among friends and colleagues (James Watt, Joseph Priestley, and Erasmus Darwin were among the Lunar Society's most illustrious members). At the same time great national societies and associations also flourished, many of them still maintaining a strong influence today. The Royal Society of London (founded in 1662) and the Paris Academy of Sciences (founded in 1666) were among the most prestigious. The Berlin Academy (founded in 1700) and the St. Petersburg Academy (founded in 1724) were also highly respected. On the other side of the Atlantic, the American Philosophical Society (founded in Philadelphia by Benjamin Franklin in 1743) offered the first regularly meeting organization for that recently settled region's scientific thinkers.

As is still the case today, funding was always a precarious matter. Following the style of the Paris Academy, the academies at Berlin and St. Petersburg were composed primarily of small, elite groups of scientists, financed by the monarch and subject to the vagaries of the government's whim for their support. The London and Philadelphia societies were self-supporting, dependent on the private financing of participating scientists and other interested individuals.

The societies, large and small, formal and informal, formed important instruments in the spread of science during the 18th century. They not only provided an organization through which members could meet and exchange the newest scientific information, but most also published papers and journals, providing a wider distribution of scientific findings.

Priestley was curious and enthusiastic with his experiments, but he was not very orderly or methodical in what he chose to do. (A great believer in the role of chance in his work, he liked to say that if he had known any chemistry, he would never have made any discoveries.) But what he did do, he observed very carefully. As a result, as 19th-century chemist Humphry Davy once remarked, "No single person ever discovered so many new and curious substances." The list includes ammonia, sulfur dioxide, carbon monoxide, hydrogen chloride, nitric oxide, and hydrogen sulfide.

And one other: oxygen. In 1774 Priestley used a burning lens with a diameter of 12 inches and a focal distance of 20 inches to

In addition the societies became valuable in promoting international communications within the scientific community

By the later 18th century, various societies such as the Manchester Literary and Philosophical Society (founded in 1781) and the Royal Society of Edinburgh (founded in 1739 and chartered in 1783) began to fill the need for organizations that could accommodate members geographically distanced from the major world cities. In addition, after the early 1800s, more specialized societies such as the Linnaean Society (founded in 1788), the Geological Society (founded in 1807), the Astronomical Society (founded in 1820), and the Chemical Society (founded in 1841) filled the need for more focused and specialized interests.

In many ways the precursor to today's scientific societies, the Royal Institution of Great Britain (founded in 1799) began to break traditions by functioning not only as a scientific society but also as a promoter of scientific events and lectures aimed at educating the average citizen in the theories and workings of science. The British Association for the Advancement of Science (founded in 1831) also furthered this endeavor by offering a spectacularly successful series of popular meetings featuring world-class scientists and attended by large audiences of middle-class interested spectators.

These associations all were intended to further the interests and traditions of scientific research, but their founders usually also had additional objectives in mind, often political, religious, or, in the case of the later societies of the Industrial Revolution, economic. Although rarely pure guardians of an idealized autonomous scientific tradition, these societies nonetheless provided a priceless forum for exchange of information and encouragement of progress in the sciences.

extract a gas from mercuric oxide. The new "air," which seemed somehow purer than normal air, caused a candle to burn brightly and vigorously. He tried the effects of breathing the new air—on mice, on plants, and even on himself. He found breathing it "peculiarly light and easy." Clinging to the phlogiston theory, he called this new air dephlogisticated air, the natural reverse of the name given by Black to the strange, non-life-supporting air that he had found, since its properties seemed to be exactly the reverse.

Unknown to Priestley, meanwhile, Carl Wilhelm Scheele [SHAY-le] (1742–86), a Swedish chemist, had already discovered the same gas, but news of his discovery had not been published. In fact the two deserve equal credit, since they both made the discovery independently.

In 1780 Priestley moved to Birmingham, where he antagonized the residents with his theology but found a stimulating and supportive group of scientific friends known as the Lunar Society. This group, partly organized by Erasmus Darwin (1731–1802), grandfather of the evolutionist Charles Darwin, met informally at dinner gatherings in each other's houses for congenial discussions of science. It became one of the most stimulating forerunners of the "think tank" in history, meeting on the night of the full moon each month so everyone could find the way home in the dark Birmingham countryside. James Watt, inventor of the steam engine and friend of Joseph Black, was there. Erasmus Darwin, always a controversial talker, often came. At the center of the group was Matthew Boulton, Watt's partner, whose optimism, commercial skill, and enthusiasm for steam power provided one of the moving forces of the Industrial Revolution. The discussions usually began about 2:00 P.M. and continued until 8:00 P.M. For Priestley and the others, the lively, informed discussions of the problems of phlogiston and heat; of the composition of water; and of metallurgy, electricity, and astronomy served as a constant spur to work.

Joseph Priestley was one of two scientists (the other was Carl Wilhelm Scheele) to discover oxygen, which he called "dephlogisticated air." *(Courtesy, Burndy Library)*

Priestley built an elaborate laboratory in Birmingham, reputed to be one of the best outfitted in Europe (though this may be an exaggeration), with all the latest equipment, no doubt assembled in consultation with his talented new friends. He worked quickly and wrote up his results by the fire at home, surrounded by his children—probably not the best way to concentrate, but he thought that isolating himself to write was antisocial. "My manner," he wrote, "has always been to give my whole attention to a subject till I have satisfied myself with respect to it, and then think no more about the matter. I hardly ever look into any thing that I have published, and when I do, it sometimes appears quite new to me. . . ."

Ironically, on the day of Lavoisier's untimely death, Priestley was heading for safety in America after rioting antirevolutionaries burned his house for his sympathy for the revolutionaries in France. Already a friend of Benjamin Franklin, he also became friends with Thomas Jefferson and found an oasis from persecution in the United States. He turned down offers of positions from the Unitarian Church and a professorship of chemistry at the University of Pennsylvania, spending the last 10 years of his life quietly writing.

Lavoisier and the Death of Phlogiston

The 19th-century German chemist Justus von Liebig once said that Antoine-Laurent Lavoisier "discovered no new body, no new property, no natural phenomenon previously unknown. His immortal glory consists in this—he infused into the body of science a new spirit."

Known as the founder of modern chemistry, Lavoisier instilled in his colleagues a new respect for quantitative techniques, the foundation of all progress in the field. While Black and Cavendish both instituted the use of careful quantitative analysis, Lavoisier succeeded in convincing other chemists of their importance. He did for chemistry what Galileo did for physics: introduced sound methodology, empiricism, and a quantitative approach.

In a demonstration about how important this quantitative approach was, in 1799 Joseph-Louis Proust discovered the law of definite proportions—the idea that whole units were being exchanged during chemical reactions. It was an early hint of the new theories about the atom, soon to come. For example, a compound might contain two elements in the ration of 4 to 1, but never in the ratio of 3.9 to 1 or 4.2 to 1, and so on. One element might combine in different proportions with other elements to produce different compounds. But each of those compounds would still obey the law of definite proportions. Carbon dioxide, for example, is made up of carbon and oxygen in proportions by weight of 3 to 8. Carbon monoxide (made up of the same elements in different proportions) is composed of carbon and oxygen in proportions by weight of 3 to 4. This quantitative discovery would prove a keystone to modern chemistry in the future.

Lavoisier was a mover in the scientific world; although his money came, to be sure, from the Fermiers Généraux, he spent it lavishly in the interest of science, and his private laboratory was a meeting place for all the major scientific figures of Europe. Thomas Jefferson and Benjamin Franklin both were warmly welcomed there. Lavoisier's wife, Marie-Anne, who married him when she was only 14, attended these meetings and wrote about them, illustrated them for Lavoisier's books, and was always deeply involved in this work. She translated works from English for him, took notes, and participated actively.

Between 1772 and 1774, Lavoisier engaged in a series of experiments and demonstrations under controlled conditions in which he tried burning various substances, including diamonds, phosphorus, sulfur, tin, and lead. He burned both tin and lead in closed vessels. When these substances are heated, it had long been known, they change color and the resulting substance, known as calx, weighs more than the original metal. But when Lavoisier weighed the whole vessel in these cases, including all that was inside—air, metal, calx, and the vessel itself—he found that the weight was unchanged. This meant that some part of the whole system must have lost weight, probably the air. (He discounted the idea held by some that phlogiston had negative weight.) If the air lost something, then at least a partial vacuum must exist inside the closed vessel. Sure enough, when he opened the vessel, air rushed in. When he weighed the vessel and its contents again, it weighed more than the original. So calx must have been formed through a combination of air with metal. Hence rusting (and combustion) was a process that did not involve the loss of phlogiston; instead what occurred was a gain from the air.

The phlogiston theory was dead. The Lavoisiers organized a grand party, and, in a dramatic ceremony with Marie-Anne Lavoisier dressed as a priestess, they burned Stahl's book on phlogiston to demonstrate the end of its grip on the science of chemistry.

Recognized as the founder of modern chemistry, Lavoisier was an energetic experimenter and an able communicator. *(Figuier,* Vies des savants, *1870)*

One other important result had come from Lavoisier's experiment: He also uncovered a basic principle—the law of conservation of mass, which became a "bulwark of chemistry" in the 19th century. (It was a concept that Einstein would further refine in the 20th century.)

Then, in October 1774, Priestley visited Lavoisier and explained his experiments with dephlogisticated air. Lavoisier listened with interest and realized suddenly that Priestley had isolated one part of air—that the air is made up largely of two gasses, one that encourages combustion and respiration, and the other that does not. The phlogiston idea, as he had already concluded, was a red herring. Now the real truth seemed clear: Priestley had isolated the gas in the air that supported burning; the new gas that Priestley found was undiluted by the portion of the air in which objects did not burn. In 1779 Lavoisier announced that air is composed of two gases, the first of which—the one that supported burning—he called *oxygen* (from Greek roots meaning "to give rise to acids"—since Lavoisier thought oxygen was contained in all acids, one of the rare occa-

Scientists often attended gatherings hosted by the Lavoisiers at which Antoine gave demonstrations while Marie Anne kept detailed notes about the experiments. *(Courtesy of Parke-Davis Division of Warner-Lambert Company)*

Lecture-demonstrations in chemistry at the Jardin du Roi in Paris—especially those given by Guillaume François Rouelle—were presented with great flair. One of Rouelle's most famous students was Antoine Lavoisier. *(Figuier,* Vies des savants, *1870)*

sions when he was wrong). The name stuck. The other gas he called *azote,* meaning "no life" in Greek. But in 1790 it was renamed nitrogen, which is the name by which it is known today.

In a low moment Lavoisier tried to downplay the fact that these insights had come to his attention through Priestley. He thought of Priestley as a mere tinkerer who did not know what he was doing; after all, he had not devoted his life to chemistry as Lavoisier had. Maybe he held some nationalistic animosity against Priestley and possibly a little political antagonism, but most likely, more than anything, Lavoisier wanted to be remembered for discovering an element, which he never succeeded in doing. He did, however, interpret what Priestley had found. He played the role of theoretician and interpreter to Priestley's laboratory work, a kind of experimental-theoretical teamwork that has become more and more important in chemistry as the results of the experiments become more and more complex.

Lavoisier also clarified Cavendish's work, repeating his experiment burning the flammable gas he had found in air and forming water. Lavoisier named this gas *hydrogen,* meaning "to give rise to water" in Greek. This also fitted well with the picture he had been putting together of the new chemistry. Animals ate substances containing

Lavoisier demonstrating the composition of air (*Figuier,* Vies des savants, *1870)*

carbon and hydrogen, inhaled oxygen, combined them, forming carbon dioxide and water, both of which they exhaled during respiration (see chapter 8). Here again, unfortunately, Lavoisier's character flaw reappeared, and he tried to snatch the credit from Cavendish for his discovery.

The new chemistry, though, began to catch on. Although Priestley, Cavendish, and Hutton never did let go of the phlogiston theory, Black aligned his thinking with Lavoisier's and so did several others.

Asked to help write an article on the history of chemistry for an encyclopedia, Lavoisier saw that the problem with discussing chemistry through the ages is that the names of substances change from country to country and from age to age. What chemistry needed was an international nomenclature (see box) that consistently reflected the composition of substances—not here a use, there a color, there a poetic fancy. So Lavoisier did for chemistry what Linnaeus had done for biology (as will be discussed in chapter 6): He established a systematic nomenclature. With two other chemists he published *Methods of Chemical Nomenclature* in 1787, establishing a clear and logical system of names that reflects composition, a system that received almost immediate acclaim (except for a few phlogiston holdouts) and is still in use today.

In 25 years Lavoisier had established quantitative measurement as the basic tool of the chemist, killed phlogiston, established the law of conservation of mass, and set up a new system of chemical nomenclature.

With Lavoisier's death in 1794, his part in the great revolution in chemistry came to a conclusion, but progress did not end there. From the foundations laid by Lavoisier, Black, Scheele, Priestley,

The Language of Chemistry

The language we use every day is full of inconsistencies, double meanings, and imprecision; that is part of the fun and beauty of language, that it can be bent and played with, made rich with analogy or funny with puns or graceful with embellishments. But for science, clarity and precision are essential. Not until chemists could eliminate imprecision in the language they used would their science truly become modern.

In 1787, when Lavoisier and his colleagues took a look at the language used in chemistry, they found a hodgepodge of confusion. The old alchemical and chemical texts drew from many languages—Greek, Hebrew, Arabic, and Latin—and named substances based on a variety of analogies and impressions. Sulfur and mercury were called "father" and "mother." "Spanish green" meant copper acetate. Chemical reaction, by analogy, was called "gestation."

The new terminology was designed to reduce confusion, and the most significant aspect of its design was Lavoisier's idea that the names of the elements in a compound should be reflected in its name. So *flowers of zinc* became *zinc oxide* (composed of zinc and oxygen), and *oil of vitriol* became *sulfuric acid*. The system also indicated relative proportions of the elements in a compound: sulfurous acid contains less oxygen than sulfuric acid, and when combined with the oxides of metals, the resulting compounds are, respectively, sulfites and sulfates.

This transformation of chemical nomenclature played a key role in the Scientific Revolution in chemistry during the 18th century—and the part Lavoisier played is one of the reasons he is considered the founder of modern chemistry.

**Normal Processes
of Science**

Experimentation
Observation

The study of the relationships
among the gases (pnuematic
chemistry) produced data.
Some scientists put forth the
phlogiston theory to explain
combustion/oxidation.

Anomalies

When iron rusts it
gains in weight.
Why?

**Paradigm Shift
and Breakthrough**

Lavoisier overturns the
phlogiston theory

Even an incorrect theory can
be scientific: Phlogiston
raised questions.
When examined carefully,
a new theory emerged that
offered better answers.

Adjustments to the phlogiston
theory attempted to explain
inconsistencies.

The Self-Correcting Nature of Science

The phlogiston theory and its demise provide an excellent illustration of science's
ability to self-correct. Scientists try ideas on for size, but if a hypothesis does not fit
new facts as they are discovered, then it is either time to adjust the hypothesis or
look at the results another way and come up with a new hypothesis.

Cavendish, and, in a way, even Stahl, chemists in the 19th century
were able to build an ever-more-accurate understanding of chemical
elements, their nature, how they react with one another, and what
processes take place in those reactions. John Dalton (1766–1844)
would build on Lavoisier and Black's quantitative analysis and wed
it with the ancient Greek Democritus's atom to come up with the
first quantitative atomic theory in 1803. In 1869 Dmitry Mendeleyev
would classify the known chemical elements into the periodic table.
At the end of the century, Marie and Pierre Curie would discover
radiation. In the process the basis would be laid for theories of the
electron and quantum mechanics.

Meanwhile many of the same individuals who had done so
much to bring chemistry into the modern era were also making
exciting discoveries in physics.

5

The Mysteries of
Heat and Electricity

NEWTON'S TAKE ON THE LAWS of physics—on gravity in particular—had received a big boost from the great expedition to measure the Earth's bulge in the early 18th century. Meanwhile, great
headway took place in two realms of physics that would soon power
the transformations brought on by the Industrial Revolution: the
physics of heat and apparent magic of electricity.

What Is Heat?

Heat had always been one of the big mysteries in physics, one that
no one had come close to resolving at the end of the 17th century.
The ancient Greeks had put forth three basic ideas about its
nature—that it was a substance, that it was a quality, and that it
was an accident of common matter (a consequence of the motion
of particles)—and versions of the first and last of these, especially,
still competed for dominance in the 18th century. It was a difficult
concept to grasp, and one of the reasons was that no one had yet
found a way to measure quantities, or degrees, of heat.

So the first hurdle was to come up with a good system of measurement, providing a way to make quantitative comparisons of heat
in different circumstances. In 1708 Ole Roemer [OHL-ay RUHR-mer]
(1644–1710), a Danish astronomer, was the first to recognize that a
thermometer needed two fixed points, and he set two observable temperatures to mark the top and bottom of this range—the point at which

The Fahrenheit Story

Most people know that wild mushrooms may be poisonous, but Daniel Fahrenheit's parents found out the hard way—when young Fahrenheit was only 15, they both died from choosing the wrong mushrooms to eat. As wards of the city council of Gdansk in Poland, where they lived, Daniel and his three siblings all went to foster homes, and Daniel was apprenticed to a shopkeeper. There he learned bookkeeping and had an opportunity to travel to Amsterdam.

In Amsterdam he saw his first thermometer—which had been invented in Florence only 60 years earlier. Fahrenheit was fascinated and decided to try his hand at fashioning thermometers of his own. As a ward of the city, he had an obligation to return home—so he was on the lam for some nine years until he came of age at 24. Traveling throughout Europe he talked to scientists about the instruments that interested him. He discovered that most thermometers had arbitrary scales that had no standardization. "Hot" was determined by the temperature on the hottest day of the year in Florence, where the existing thermometers were made. "Cold" was marked on the coldest day of the year. Fahrenheit realized that he needed to find substances that changed form at a particular temperature. Then temperature could have the same meaning from one thermometer to another. By the time he was 28, he had succeeded in making two thermometers that gave exactly the same reading when they were in the same location. It was a first, and Daniel Fahrenheit continued to use universal properties of particular substances to create fine, accurate thermometers—the first of their kind.

snow melts at one end and the temperature at which water boils at the other. Daniel Fahrenheit (1686–1736), from the Netherlands, used Roemer's scale, with some adaptations, for thermometers he designed in 1714, substituting mercury for alcohol. This meant that temperatures above water's boiling point could be measured because mercury has a much higher boiling point than alcohol. The Swedish astronomer Anders Celsius (1701–44), meanwhile, used the same fixed points, separating them by 100 units for the centigrade scale he devised in 1742. A compatriot, biologist Carolus Linnaeus, inverted his thermometer, setting the boiling point at 100 and the freezing point at zero, the arrangement still used today on the Celsius thermometer (also known as centigrade), used by scientists all over the world.

In the 18th century the favored theory of heat was established by Hermann Boerhaave (1668–1738), who thought of heat as a special sort of matter. This doctrine fitted in well with the theory of phlogiston (see chapter 4), which, like light and electricity, was thought to be an "imponderable," or weightless, fluid. Although Lavoisier demolished the theory of phlogiston, he continued to think of heat as a fluid that could be poured from one substance to another, and he named it *caloric*, including it in his *Traité élémentaire de chimie* (Elements of chemistry), published in 1789. It was a theory that served the 18th century well, and by the end of the century Pierre-Simon Laplace (see chapter 2) had incorporated the concept of caloric in a new, complex general picture of matter. His mathematical analysis greatly contributed to the prestige of the theory.

Dr. Black and His Friend James Watt

In the 1760s Scottish chemistry professor Joseph Black also became interested in the nature of heat. The question loomed particularly large in industrial Glasgow and Edinburgh, where the union of Scotland and England in 1707 had produced a healthy economy with good markets for the local whiskey industry. The big distilleries used large amounts of fuel and generated huge amounts of heat to turn liquids into vapors; then those huge amounts of heat had to be removed to condense into vapors; then those huge amounts of heat had to be removed to condense vapors back into liquids. To manage the distilleries economically, knowing the exact amount of heat involved in these processes was an absolute necessity. In fact the

English chemist Joseph Black was the first to isolate and demonstrate the properties of carbon dioxide (which he called "fixed air"). *(Courtesy, Burndy Library)*

need to remove great quantities of heat from the vapor had a direct effect on the profitability of a distillery.

Black often said he could not understand why the distillery managers had never paid much attention to the scientific principles involved, when those principles clearly had such an important impact on their livelihood. But this relationship between pure science and technological advancement is traditionally too little recognized and much too little supported. Even today research and development departments are nearly always the first to be cut back when a business is trimming its costs, and universities are always a target for budget reductions in lean times.

Black did not ever publish his lectures, in which he discussed his ideas most thoroughly, but his editor, John Robison, published material from Black's notebooks and his own observation:

> Since a fine winter day of sunshine did not at once clear the hills of snow, nor a frosty night suddenly cover the ponds with a thick cake of ice, Dr. Black was already convinced that much heat was absorbed and fixed in the water which slowly trickled from the wreaths of snow; and on the other hand, that much heat emerged from it while it was slowly changing into ice. For, during a thaw, a thermometer will always sink when removed from the air into melting snow; and during severe frost it will rise when plunged into freezing water. Therefore, in the first case, the snow is receiving heat, and in the last, the water is allowing it to emerge again.

In 1762, at a meeting of the University Philosophical Club, a group of professors that met informally in Glasgow, Black discussed his insights further. Ice does not change temperature when it melts, he pointed out, but material in the vicinity of the ice gets cooler, even though the temperature of the ice does not get warmer. What happens to the heat? Does it disappear? Fahrenheit had once observed that water could be cooled below the temperature of melting snow without freezing, although any disturbance of water cooled in this way caused it to immediately freeze rock solid. When this happened the temperature actually rose! So, as the water froze, that is, as it changed state from liquid to solid, it gave off heat. Water, Black saw, remains liquid because it contains a certain amount of heat; when the heat is removed, the fluidity disappears, and instead of liquid water you have solid ice. Because the heat present in the fluid water did not register on a thermometer, Black called it "latent" heat, to indicate that it was present but not measurable by the usual means.

Black also figured out a way to measure this latent heat. He measured the amount of heat required to melt a certain quantity of ice. Then he applied that amount of heat to the water produced by the melted ice and found that its temperature rose 140° F.

Between 1762 and 1764 Black worked on the natural extension of the concept of latent heat in ice—the idea that something similar must happen when water is converted to stream. He found that it took about five times as long, with fire at the same strength, to transform boiling water to steam as it did to bring water to the boiling point.

At this point some extra help and a new friend entered the picture: James Watt, an instrument maker for the university. Watt devised apparatus for demonstrations and experimental proofs of the latent-heat concept for Black's classes, and based on the theoretical insights he gained from Black, Watt succeeded in inventing a new apparatus for a steam engine he was repairing: a separate condenser. This single invention turned out to be the key to making steam engines efficient enough to become economical sources of energy for both transportation and industry. Fueled by coal or coke, James Watt's practical steam engine freed factories to be located anywhere, away from the riverside locations they had needed for water power. The steam engine soon became a cheap source of power for nearly every industry, from coal mining to ironworks to textile plants (and in the following century, railways and steamships).

Black was enormously pleased and loved to tell his students about Watt's accomplishments. When Watt took out a patent in 1769, he was on his way to well-deserved rewards. "Dr. Black," wrote Robison, "would scarcely have been more gratified, had those advantages accrued to himself. . . . both the friends considered that period of successful investigation as among the most fertile of enjoyment of any part of their lives."

Earlier Black had also showed that equal masses of different substances require different ("specific") quantities of heat to bring them to the same temperature. Or, put another way, when equal weights of two different substances are brought to equilibrium from two different temperatures, the equilibrium temperature is not necessarily at the midpoint. That is, the same quantity of heat applied to the two different substances produces a characteristic temperature change for each substance. Black was a subscriber to the fluid theory of heat, and

A high-pressure tram engine, designed by Richard Trevithick, probably similar to the steam carriage he built in 1801, based on James Watt's steam engine (*Samuel Smiles,* The Life of George Stephenson and of His Son Robert Stephenson, *1868*)

as he began to work out what he called "specific" heats for various substances, he became more convinced than ever that the dynamical or kinetic theory of heat proposed by Bacon (and later reframed by Rumford) was inconsistent with the existence of specific heats. Unfortunately this opinion turned out to be an example of how sound science can sometimes seem to fail to corroborate a valid theory.

Count Rumford and Heat as Motion

The man called Count Rumford began life as Benjamin Thompson, born in 1753 in Woburn, Massachusetts. It was the beginning of a strange and eccentric life, not always honorable, but definitely interesting. As a youngster he nearly killed himself making explosives for a celebration of the repeal of the Stamp Act while working at a local retail shop in Salem. He then worked awhile at another retail store in Boston after his recovery, and at 19 he married a rich widow. He moved with her to an estate in Rumford (now Concord), New Hampshire, but the situation became complicated when the Revolutionary War broke out and Thompson began spying on his neighbors for the British. Presumably things were getting a little uncomfortable around home, so he hopped a British military ship heading out of Boston, leaving his wife and child behind.

While in England, Thompson worked for the British secretary of state for the colonies (where his knowledge of America was much appreciated) and became acquainted with Sir Joseph Banks, then president of the Royal Society. Through Banks, Thompson met the leading scientists of the day.

He returned to the colonies before the end of the war, however, as a lieutenant colonel in the king's forces. Unfortunately for him the British lost. He was forced into permanent exile, leaving immediately for England, where his opportunistic character emerged again as he took bribes and possibly even spied against the British for the French.

In 1783 he received permission from George III to head for the Continent, where he went to work for Elector Karl Theodor of Bavaria. There he served well in various administrative positions,

The Newcomen Engine and the Industrial Revolution

One of the most important discoveries of the early 18th century was that coke, made from coal, could be substituted for charcoal, made out of wood, to power blast furnaces. The blast furnaces produced pig and cast iron for manufacturing, but, prior to the discovery that coke could be used for fuel, each furnace could consume as much as 200 acres of valuable wood for each year's operation. The discovery, generally attributed to the Quaker iron master Abraham Darby in 1709, had its first practical application in production at his furnaces in Coalbrookdale, Shropshire, England, where Darby manufactured iron boilers for the Newcomen engine invented in 1712. The engine, invented by the English blacksmith Thomas Newcomen, helped to pave the way for the Industrial Revolution. The simple device, using a jet of cold water to condense steam entering a cylinder, created atmospheric pressure to drive pistons. By 1733 the engine was in wide use to pump water out of coal mines, allowing for the greater production of coal from flooded colliery galleries.

including minister of war and state councilor. He set up workhouses for the homeless, introduced Watt's steam engine and the potato to the Continent, and accomplished other positive goals. The elector was pleased, and Thompson became a count of the Holy Roman Empire in 1791, choosing to use the name Rumford, probably out of nostalgia for the estate he had left behind in New Hampshire.

While in Bavaria, Rumford, who had always been interested in science, became deeply involved with the nature of heat. While boring a cannon in Munich in 1798, he observed that the metal got very hot as the boring machine chiseled the hole—so hot that it had to be cooled with water. Caloric-theory backers would explain this by saying that the weightless caloric fluid was being released from the metal as the shavings were scraped away. But Rumford noticed that the heat never let up as long as the boring continued, and if one measured the amount of caloric released during the boring, the total would be enough to melt the metal if (somehow) it were poured back into the brass. He also noticed that if he used instruments so dull that no shavings were cut from the metal, the metal got even hotter—not less so, as would be expected if it was the process of breaking up the metal that caused the release of caloric.

So Rumford suggested a kinetic theory of heat, namely, that the mechanical motion of the boring tool was converted into heat. Heat, therefore, he said, was a form of motion. It was an idea hinted at before him by Francis Bacon, Robert Boyle, and Robert Hooke.

Rumford's idea would soon gain some strong adherents, who rejected the caloric theory in favor of the kinetic. But, as the century closed, caloric theory remained the favorite of most physicists

Benjamin Thompson, later known as Count Rumford, led a peripatetic life that began in America and ended in England and France. He is best remembered for his inquiries into the nature of heat. *(Edgar Fahs Smith Collection–University of Pennsylvania Library)*

and chemists—no doubt still influenced by the powerful opinion of Antoine Lavoisier and by the mathematical support for caloric. But Rumford, it turned out, was right, though it would not be shown until James Joule (1818–89) was able to provide a mathematical quantity for how much heat was produced by a given quantity of mechanical energy.

Rumford returned to England in 1798, the negative aspects of his character finally having worn thin in Bavaria. In England he was admitted to the Royal Society for his achievements and founded the Royal Institution that same year. Thomas Young and Humphry Davy, two rising young physicists, became lecturers there, and Davy, in particular, was enthusiastic about Rumford's kinetic theory, publishing results of an experiment he had done that he thought supported it. But most physicists remained unconvinced until James Maxwell finally established kinetic theory in 1871, more than 70 years later.

In 1804 Rumford (whose first wife had died) married Lavoisier's widow, Marie-Anne, who was wealthy and, of course, famous (she kept Lavoisier's name after her marriage to Rumford). He was 50, she about 47. But the marriage did not go well; they began to quarrel immediately and they lasted together only four years, with Rumford muttering that Lavoisier was lucky to have been guillotined. Rumford, as one historian put it, was no daisy but did come out smelling like a rose, at least from his point of view—he walked away with half of Marie-Anne Lavoisier's fortune.

Rumford's American daughter by his first wife joined him in 1811 and looked after him in his later years. Also, though he was a crusty and often unscrupulous character, in addition to the contributions his work made to science, he also contributed numerous practical inventions—including a double boiler, a drip coffee pot, and a cooking range—that he purposely left unpatented (free to be used). He also left most of his estate to the United States when he died in 1814, as well as an endowment for a professorship in applied science at Harvard University.

Electricity: The Great Parlor Game

People have known a little bit about electricity for a long time. A piece of amber, both the ancient Greeks and the ancient Chinese had found, would attract lightweight materials, such as a feather or a scrap of cloth, if one rubbed it. The Greeks called this fossil resin substance *elektron*. But no one knew a lot about it.

In 1600, in his book on magnetism, William Gilbert distinguished between magnetism, the power of a lodestone to attract iron, and what he called *vis electrica,* the ability of amber (and other substances he found, such as jet and sulfur) to attract objects when rubbed. He was the first to suggest that this property was not intrinsic to the amber, jet, and sulfur, but was a fluid, either produced or transferred by the rubbing. But he did not discuss the *vis electrica* much because he thought it was trivial.

Electricity remained trivial for a long time. In the 17th century the Irish scientist Robert Boyle enjoyed a pleasant diversion as much as anyone, and he recounted noticing

> . . . that false locks of hair, brought to a certain degree of dryness, will be attracted by the flesh of some persons. I had proof in two beautiful ladies who wore them; for at some times, I observed that they could not keep them from flying to their cheeks, and from sticking there, though neither of them had occasion for or did use paints.

Boyle's contemporary, Otto von Guericke of Magdeburg in Saxony, carried out electrical experiments using a rotating sphere of sulfur as an electrical machine. Created by fusing sulfur and other minerals inside a glass globe used as a mold and later removed, this machine was "as large as an infant's head." To provide an axis on which to spin it, von Guericke bored a hole through the center through which he inserted an iron rod with a handle attached to turn it. Holding one hand against the globe, he could crank it with the other, and the friction electrified the sphere, which would then attract other objects. Von Guericke found that he could transfer this electricity to other objets, such as another ball of sulfur. He also noticed another interesting point: The objects that were initially attracted to the sulfur globe were repelled by it once they touched it.

By the 18th century the use of electrified glass globes and rods became a party diversion all over Europe. Guests amused themselves in shocking each other; moving light objects, such as feathers; and making each other's hair stand on end.

Naturally scientists wondered what caused this phenomenon. They suspected that it probably was another "imponderable" fluid—as many of them also classified heat and phlogiston, the substance

Experiments with electricity were both entertaining—when they were not dangerous—and instructive. *(Edgar Fahs Smith Collection–University of Pennsylvania Library)*

thought to cause combustion. To explain the attraction/repulsion that von Guericke had noticed, the most popular theory was a two-fluid theory. One fluid repelled; the other attracted. Rubbing a glass rod or globe with fur transferred some of the fluids, creating the electrical charge. Opposite fluids then attracted each other (in the same way opposite poles attract in magnets).

One of the first breakthroughs came in 1729, when Stephen Gray found that when he electrified a long glass tube with corks at either end, not only the tube but also the corks became electrified. He had discovered electrical conduction. Also, a contraption called the Leyden jar, after Leiden (Leyden) in the Netherlands, led to even more fruitful experimentation. It was invented in about 1745 by independent inventors in the Netherlands and Pomerania. It was a glass jar coated with metal both inside and out, and it was basically a storage container (named a "capacitor" a half-century later by Alessandro Volta) that could store large quantities of static electrical charges produced through friction. If one wanted to discharge (cause the electricity to be released from) a charged Leyden jar, all one had to do was bring one's hand near the center rod, and in the early days of electrical research, this brought many a researcher a nasty jolt. A piece of metal brought near the jar would cause tiny jagged sparks to jump across the gap, giving off sharp, crackling noises.

Like the glass globes and the glass rods, the Leyden jar became a great conversation piece at social gatherings. But its invention also marked the beginning of serious research on the nature and characteristics of electricity.

Benjamin Franklin, Electrical Diplomat

American scientist Benjamin Franklin (1706–90) was known throughout the world by the time of his death as a national leader in his country, an international diplomat, an ingenious inventor, and a weaver of homespun wisdom. He was also world-renowned for his fertile and stimulating mind—he was friends with many European scientists, including Priestley and Lavoisier—and, especially, his work with electricity, some of it exceedingly risky.

When he retired from his business a wealthy man at 42, Franklin was free to become even more involved in the electrical studies he had begun as early as 1746. He developed a theory that frictional electricity involved a transfer of "electric fluid," leaving surfaces "positive" or "negative." Positive charge was most likely an extra amount of fluid, and negative charge would be a shortage of it. Although the fluid theory did not last long beyond the 18th century, the idea of positive and negative charges did. This "one-fluid theory" broke with the commonly accepted "two-fluid theory."

Franklin also recognized the law of conservation of charge, which says that for every negative charge created, there must be an equal amount of positive charge. Also, all negative and positive charges in the universe must balance perfectly. So if one rubs a balloon against a wool sweater, the balloon picks up a negative charge—but it also leaves a positive charge on the sweater. Then when one places the balloon on the wall, it will stay in place because its negative charge attracts the slight positive charge already present in the wall. Along with Franklin's one-fluid theory, the law of conservation of charge helped explain what made the recently invented Leyden jar work.

The Leyden jar's capacity for accumulating greater charges made possible all kinds of experiments, uses, and stunts—and Franklin was delighted with it ("that wonderful bottle . . . that miraculous jar!" he once remarked). So much so that in 1749 Franklin and his friends decided to throw a party on the banks of the Schuykill River. The party's theme was electricity, its uses and wonders. They planned to send a spark across the river through the water, kill a turkey by electric shock (which tenderized the meat), and roast it on a fire kindled by the "Electrified Bottle." The day ended, however, on a shocking note, as Franklin recounted in a letter to his brother John:

> Being about to kill a turkey from the shock of two large glass jars, containing as much electrical fire as forty common phials, I inadvertently took the whole through my own arms and body, by receiving the fire from the united top wires with one hand, while the other held a chain connected with the outsides of both jars. The company present (whose talking to me, and to one another, I suppose occasioned my inattention to what I was about) say that the flash was very great and the crack as loud as a pistol: yet, my senses being instantly gone, I neither saw the one nor heard the other; nor did I feel the stroke on my hands. . . . I then felt what I know not well how to describe, a universal blow throughout my whole body from head to foot, which seemed within as well as without; after which the first

thing I took notice of was a violent quick shaking of my body, which gradually remitting, my senses as gradually returned.

The crack and crackle and the jagged shape of the sparks set Franklin to pondering the relationship between the static electricity in the Leyden jar and the lightning in the sky, which led him to his most famous (and dangerous) experiment. In a thunderstorm in 1752, he flew a kite that had been especially prepared with a pointed wire attached to a silk thread (silk conducts an electrical charge very well). The idea was that the silk thread would conduct the electricity

The Enterprising Mr. Franklin

In addition to his active scientific and political pursuits, Benjamin Franklin was also America's first major publisher. Beginning in 1732, his *Poor Richard's Almanack* continued through 25 editions over the next 25 years, becoming in its time the most popular publication (after the Bible) in the colonies. An agricultural handbook, the *Almanack* was chock-full of recipes, casual and useful information on such subjects as health and personal hygiene, and down-home, folksy sayings usually attributed to "Richard Saunders," in reality Franklin himself.

Reorganizing the rough-and-tumble colonial postal service after becoming postmaster general, Franklin improved the circulation of his *Almanack,* as well as mail service in general, by doubling and tripling postal service in rural areas, increasing the speed of delivery, and improving roads from Maine to Georgia into a system that became known as the King's Highway.

His success in business, including such practical inventions as the Franklin stove, allowed him to retire in 1748, intending to devote the remainder of his life to his scientific pursuits. These included his famous experiments with electricity, as well as ideas about light that rejected the particle theory and foreshadowed the work of Thomas Young in the early 19th century.

After founding the American Philosophical Society in 1743, he also founded, in 1749, a college that would later become the University of Pennsylvania. He traveled to Britain as the agent of the Pennsylvania Assembly in 1757 and crisscrossed the Atlantic numerous times, attending meetings of the Royal Society, while at the same time campaigning for the indefrom the sky (assuming there was electricity in the sky) to the ground, where Franklin had attached a metal key. He watched the sky for the right moment, then, as he saw lightning flickering in the clouds, he reached his hand up to the key. A spark leaped across the gap just as the spark from the Leyden jar did. Franklin also was able to charge the Leyden jar from the lightning. He had proved that lightning was electrical in nature, and he was elected to the Royal Society in London.

Franklin was, however, extraordinarily lucky. The next two men who tried to duplicate his experiment were killed.

pendence of the American colonies as their foremost spokesman in Britain.

Franklin is perhaps best known as one of the drafters of the American Declaration of Independence in 1776 and one of its most famous signers. He also succeeded in securing French aid for America during a diplomatic mission to France (1777–85) and was also instrumental in the final negotiations for peace at the end of the Revolutionary War, which guaranteed America's independence in 1783.

The United States of America's first world-class figure, Franklin gained such great popularity after the war that he soon found himself once again drawn into

Benjamin Franklin had both many talents and interests—and his interest in the scientific study of electricity (as well as its entertainment value) was keen. (*Edgar Fahs Smith Collection–University of Pennsylvania Library*)

civic and political activities. He continued to serve in various capacities, including his important involvement in the ratification of the United States Constitution, until his death in 1790.

A diagram of electrical apparatuses that appeared in Franklin's scientific treatise,
*Experiments and Observations on Electricity (Edgar Fahs Smith
Collection–University of Pennsylvania Library)*

Always practical, Franklin put his experience to immediate use,
inventing the first lightning rod, and by 1782, 400 houses in
Philadelphia, where he lived, were protected by lightning rods. He

also rigged bells to ring in his house whenever charged clouds passed overhead, so that he could take the opportunity to collect electrical charges or otherwise experiment.

Coulomb's Law

Charles-Augustin de Coulomb (1736–1806) established another major electrical law in 1785. He decided to measure electrical force using two electrically charged cork balls attached to a rod that, in turn, he suspended from a wire. Nearby he placed two other cork balls having an opposite charge. He knew exactly how much charge each ball had, and he could calculate the force of attraction between balls by the amount of twist in the wire. The results amazed him and everyone else. He found that the electrical force between two charges depends on the strength of the two charges. That is, the bigger the difference between the two electrical charges, the stronger the attraction between them. Also, he found, the farther apart they are, the less the attraction. If they were twice as far apart, the attraction would be only a fourth as much; at a distance three times as far, the amount of attraction would drop to one-ninth, and so on. These observations he summed up in Coulomb's law, stating that the force between two electric charges is proportional to the product and inversely proportional to the square of the distance between the charges.

Coulomb and his colleagues were stunned to realize that this inverse square relationship exactly paralleled Newton's law of universal gravitation. Based on Coulomb's work it was clear that gravitation and electricity worked very similarly. While he was at it, Coulomb made a similar study of magnetism and found that magnetic force also follows an inverse square law—very exciting news, for it demonstrated that all three of these fundamental forces follow similar laws. The universe, indeed, must operate by a simple, neat, and orderly set of principles. As the 18th century drew to a close, physicists must have felt a sense of excitement and anticipation about discoveries to come, especially in electricity, that "trivial" subject that all of a sudden seemed to be anything but.

The twilight of the 18th century glowed with the dawning of a coming era, a time when electricity would be harnessed by humans and set to work. By 1800 Alessandro Volta, an Italian professor of physics, would invent the first electric battery, which would enable scientists to store electricity and study it more effectively under laboratory

One stormy day Franklin demonstrated that lightning is a form of electricity by using a kite and a metal key. Luckily he lived to record the results. Other experimenters did not. *(Edgar Fahs Smith Collection–University of Pennsylvania Library)*

conditions. By 1831 Michael Faraday, an English physicist and chemist, would produce electricity by moving a magnet through a coil of copper wire, producing the first electric generator dynamo.

The 18th-Century Legacy to the Physical Sciences

In the physical sciences the legacy left by the 18th century to those who followed included several quiet but nonetheless key contributions: the new recognition of the importance of quantitative analysis; the continued practice of Galileo's principles of rigorous methodology, observation, and experiment; and the development of experimental skills.

In addition theoretical and experimental advances were made by the 18th-century *philosophes* and experimentalists in every area of the physical sciences.

In astronomy the discovery of a new planet, the measurement of the distance to the Sun, and the establishment of new ideas about nebulae and galaxies all revealed that both the solar system and the universe were much larger and more complex than anyone had previously imagined.

Geologists, struggling against ideological conflicts with biblical accounts of the creation of the Earth, nonetheless made extensive studies of rock strata and other geological formations, forming a wealth of theories about the Earth's history. At the end of the century, they stood temporarily stymied by the widespread acceptance of Cuvier's theory of catastrophism, but James Hutton had already put forth the beginnings of a doctrine, uniformitarianism, that would prove more productive, at least for the moment.

The 18th century had seen a veritable Scientific Revolution in the field of chemistry, completely transforming that area of inquiry from its medieval roots. Black and Lavoisier had established new quantitative methods; Priestley, Scheele, Cavendish, Lavoisier, and others had all contributed to a transformed understanding of gases; and a new scientific nomenclature brought a much-needed precision to the language of chemistry.

In physics Newton's law of universal gravitation was validated by successful measurement of the shape of the Earth. Despite an ongoing struggle to come to grips with the nature of heat, with progress hung up on the lingering theory of heat as a fluid or "caloric," discoveries about the characteristics of heat and methods for measuring it made possible some of the technological breakthroughs of the Industrial Revolution. The 18th century also saw the first scientific studies of the phenomenon of electricity, including the invention of the first capacitor, the Leyden jar, and exploration of some of its characteristics.

Much, though, remained to be done in the physical sciences. What was the true nature of electricity? What was magnetism? What was heat? What was light? What mystery lay at the heart of chemical reactions? How far beyond our dreams did the universe really extend? Was the Earth itself young or old, and what forces had really shaped it?

The stage was set for the century to come. The wonderfully complex mystery story had many more acts. Perhaps, in fact, it never ends. For now, though, the scientific investigators of the 18th century had, through their interrogations of nature, opened up a provocative new list of questions in the physical sciences. It was the turn of the next generation of investigators now to try to find new answers. That, though, is another story.

In the life sciences, meanwhile, the spirit of the Age of Reason and the Newtonian revolution were providing new structure to complex lines of investigation.

PART II

The Life Sciences in the 18th Century

6

Linnaeus: The Great Name Giver

PLUCKED FROM THE EARLY DAYS of the 16th century and dropped into the 18th century, a bewildered time traveler would probably no longer recognize the world. The combined brilliance of the great 17th-century thinkers had changed the face of the physical universe—at least as people saw it. The Earth was no longer the center of the universe but just another planet in orbit around the Sun. The Sun itself, as well as the entire solar system, was in movement. Gone were the beautiful and perfect spheres of Aristotle and Ptolemy. The stars moved. The sky was filled with what appeared to be other galaxies, and all those, said the astronomers, were in motion. Within those galaxies, some speculated, other solar systems spun around their suns. Everything, it seemed, was movement—unceasing, mathematically predictable movement.

Only in the field of natural history—what today we call the life sciences—would the bewildered time traveler find familiar ideas. By now the physical scientists had accepted motion and not fixity, or permanence, as their guiding principle. But for those who studied living forms—the natural scientists—one ancient idea still reigned supreme at the beginning of the 18th century: the Great Chain of Being. This was the premier concept dominating early 18th-century biology: the idea that living forms, created by God, were fixed and forever the same, each and every form of life part of a grand design, like a rung on a ladder or a link in a chain.

Originating with the ancient Greeks and developed further by Christian philosophers, this idea of a Great Chain of Being held that everything that could exist already did—and had always

93

existed. That everything, from inanimate objects to living things, whether insect or fish or human, formed an unchangeable and permanent link along a chain that was arranged in a hierarchy from the lowest to the highest. Plants were higher along this chain than rocks. Animals were higher than plants, certain animals were higher than other animals, and humans were higher still. For many the chain stretched even further—beyond human to the hierarchy of angels, extending in ever-increasing perfection toward God. Each link on the chain was permanently fixed in position, and each link had an inferior on one side and a superior on the other. Each creature's position on the great chain was created by God at the beginning and could never be altered or changed. Furthermore, according to believers in this view, no new species had been created since the beginning of the universe, and none had become extinct. For either to have happened would have altered the links in the chain—an impossibility, since God had created it perfectly in the beginning.

Carl von Linné, better known by his Latinized name, Carolus Linnaeus, was a devout believer in the great chain. But as so often happens to scientists, his greatest work furthered human knowledge while working against his own beliefs. The days of the concept of the Great Chain of Being, with its insistence on permanence and immutability, were numbered, even in the 18th century, and the major work of Linnaeus—a massive, non-hierarchical system of classification—contributed in some ways to its demise.

Carolus Linnaeus, Truant Student

Born in southern Sweden on May 23, 1707, Linnaeus was the son of a poor clergyman who named his family after a gigantic linden tree that grew near his house. While Linnaeus's father hoped that his son would follow in his footsteps and prepare for the ministry, Linnaeus was not much of a student and did not show much interest in theology. He preferred to spend his days skipping classes. Not that he had no curiosity; it was just that his curiosity centered on areas not necessarily taught in school: He had fallen in love with botany.

The situation caused a good deal of stress and argument for Linnaeus at home, and as a result most of the boy's childhood was dismal. But fortunately he found a friend in the rector of the school who perceived the youngster's brightness and loaned him books on botany. A physics teacher also came to the rescue by diplomatically pointing out to Linnaeus's father that his son was bright and quick to learn when the subject interested him. The teacher also suggested the boy's interest in botany might be channeled into a career in medicine. His intervention seems to have led to a family compromise, and he even took young Linnaeus into his home and helped prepare him for entrance into the university at nearby Lund.

At Lund, however, Linnaeus did not fare well. He really had no interest in medicine. If he had, he would have been deeply disappointed. The school was in financial trouble and had only one medical instructor at the faculty. Boredom quickly set in, and once more Linnaeus began cutting his classes and taking to the fields.

Carolus Linnaeus established the first well-organized naming system for plants and animals. *(Figuier, Vies des savants, 1870)*

Fortunately, though, Linnaeus had another lucky break. He had secured boarding with a member of the faculty, Kilian Stobaeus. One night Stobaeus caught Linnaeus sneaking into the library to read the professor's botany books. When Stobaeus asked for an explanation, Linnaeus tried to assure his host that he had not intended any harm. In the process he revealed such an extensive knowledge of botany that Stobaeus gave him complete run of the library as well as his encouragement and friendship.

Despite Stobaeus's friendship, though, Linnaeus was unhappy at Lund. So bad grades and all, he drifted to the University at Uppsala, 40 miles north of Stockholm, where he was drawn by Uppsala's famous botanical gardens—but he was again disappointed. Once a proud school, Uppsala, like Lund, was also suffering through lean financial times. The botanical gardens were in terrible condition and the medical facilities were so impoverished that the school no longer even had a laboratory of its own but was reduced to holding lectures in chemistry at an apothecary shop.

By then so poor and ill fed that he was suffering from scurvy, painful headaches, and malnutrition, Linnaeus might have dropped out from Uppsala except for another fortunate meeting with an older teacher. As he was cutting class one day (a habit he had again fallen into), studying what was left of the flowers in the botanical gardens, Linnaeus bumped into a theology professor, Olaf Celsius, who had a keen avocational interest in botany. In a fortunate replay of his previous experience at Lund, instead of being lectured or reprimanded for cutting classes, Linnaeus was offered the use of Celsius's extensive botanical library.

Linnaeus's meeting with Celsius resulted in an invitation to live with the older man. He also began to make a little money tutoring other students in botany, and he was slowly starting to build a reputation among the Uppsala faculty for his botanical knowledge.

After reading a review of a paper about the sexuality of plants, Linnaeus began some studies of his own, particularly on plant stamens and pistils. The result was a short paper that he presented to Celsius as a New Year's Day present. Celsius was so impressed that he had copies made and circulated. When one of the copies was read at the Swedish Royal Academy of Science, the academy recognized its worth and ordered it to be officially printed under the academy stamp. It was Linnaeus's first taste of true accomplishment.

From that point on, Linnaeus's attitude and fortune changed dramatically. He immediately applied for and received an appointment as a lecturer on the plants in the botanical gardens.

His career was beginning to look brighter, but his sudden change in fortune may have begun to go to his head. Always individualistic, he became even more eccentric and self-centered; always pious (despite not wanting a career in the ministry) he became self-righteous and moralistic. Now, too, his ambition was burning. After years of trying to justify himself and his choices to others, he was at last accepted as a legitimate botanist.

The taste of success was sweet. So sweet, in fact, that he decided to secure it further with some dramatic achievement that would reach beyond poor, impoverished Uppsala and raise him head and shoulders above his competitors, even those with better academic credentials.

Journey to Lapland

In 1732, aided by a small grant from the Swedish government, Linnaeus set off on a field expedition to study plant life in the rugged terrain of Lapland, the far northern regions of Scandinavia, above the Arctic Circle. The experience was the most dramatic of his life, and one he referred to often whenever he wrote about himself (which was also quite often: he wrote four separate autobiographies, each different from the preceding one). For five months, poorly equipped (the entire expedition had been financed for $100) and struggling against the hostile elements, Linnaeus tramped the wild northern terrain, collecting notes and plants wherever he went. Traveling largely on foot, he slept wrapped in animal skins, which he also used as an overcoat to protect himself from the cold. He trekked up and down the river basins along the Gulf of Bothnia, working his way slowly north, wading through frigid, knee-deep water in the icy marshlands, hiking through forests, and scaling mountainsides.

All in all Linnaeus covered 4,600 square miles in northern Scandinavia, mostly on foot in the cold lands of the north, and he returned with an impressive collection of more than 100 new specimens. He also brought back a colorful Lapp costume, which he later took to wearing on public or official occasions to remind everyone of his adventures.

Returning to Uppsala, his reputation enhanced but his pocketbook still meager, he continued his lectures to ever-increasing and appreciative audiences. He was also fortunate enough to fall in love with the daughter of a wealthy doctor, who not only heartily approved of the adventurous and pious botanist but also gave him enough money to send him to a small Dutch university to finish his medical degree. It could not have been a very demanding course, since he was back, degree in hand, within a few months. In any case the degree provided backup if his career in botany ever fell apart.

By now, though, Linnaeus was fairly sure he would not need much backup.

Putting Order to Diversity

Linnaeus's adventures in Lapland, with its wide diversity of plant life, had brought him face to face with one of the oldest and most perplexing problems facing botanists and other natural historians. But Linnaeus had found a way to solve it. Returning once again to Uppsala,

Linnaeus's journey to Lapland offered frigid weather and dangerous terrain, but the specimens he gathered served to spark a solid career in life science. *(Figuier,* Vies des savants, *1870)*

he set to work on a small book that he had been planning, a book that he was sure would establish his credentials in botany once and for all.

He was right. Published in 1735, the slim volume entitled *Systema naturae* (System of nature) established a particularly methodical system of classification of living things and set him on his way to becoming the most famous scientist in Sweden, the founder of modern taxonomy. As further revised and expanded through the years, his book finally gave botanists and naturalists a way to handle one of their most vexing and perplexing problems: how to name and classify the world's life forms. For as long as people had been observing and writing about nature, they had struggled with naming specimens and showing their relationships to other specimens. The same plant, for instance, might be found in widely different areas around the world—and might be called by a different name in each area. Natural scientists and students studying the plant needed to find a way to identify it by a name that they could all use when communicating about it. Ideally the name would also convey something descriptive and useful about the specimen that would allow researchers to group similar specimens together closely enough to study their similarities and differences. It was obvious, for instance, that a dog was different from a whale: Whales lived in water and dogs did not. But how different was a dog from a cat? Both lived on land, both had fur and four feet. Dividing creatures into just two groups, those that lived on land and those that lived in water, was not helpful enough. The categories were too large and could be extremely misleading. In fact a respected scientist of Linnaeus's time had followed just such a path, grouping beavers along with fish, since both lived in water. Needless to say, that was an extremely misleading classification—so much so that the Catholic Church for a while permitted beavers to be eaten on fast days (when no meat was permitted, only fish)!

In the late 1600s English naturalist John Ray had made a little progress in resolving the growing classification problems. But in the wake of a virtual flood of new specimens of plants and animals coming in from all over the globe, as explorers and merchants continued to expand their operations, it was obvious that some new system for naming and classifying specimens was sorely needed. Only then could any serious scientific work be done on the exciting new finds.

Linnaeus knew that the system he came up with was not "natural," was not the ultimate plan of nature, and did not reflect the ultimate delineation of the Great Chain. But his chief aim was to create a system of nomenclature that was practical and easy to use. This he did with such success that much of his system, though modified, is still used today, more than 200 years later. Linnaeus grouped plants and animals into small groups he called *genera* (the plural of *genus*), and subdivided those groups into species. He also used what scientists like to call a *binary nomenclature,* a two-part (binary) system of names. Because Latin was still the international scientific language of the time, the names he gave were Latin or Latinized, and that tradition has stuck to this day. Each two-part name begins with the genus (the larger, more inclusive group), followed by the species (the smaller, more specific group). He grouped animals or plants together in one genus that seemed to have something in common (usually a structure, a body shape, or some distinctive way of reproducing, for instance). For example zebras and horses clearly have similarities, while horses and dogs have much less in common. So Linnaeus put zebras and horses in the same genus, *Equus.* Dogs, by contrast, are classified in the genus *Canis* (the same genus, by the way, as wolves). The shared genus name points to similarities in a group, but zebras and horses are also distinct from each other. So the zebra is named *Equus zebra,* while the horse goes by the name *Equus caballus*—the second part of the name, the species, emphasizing the unique aspect of different members of the genus. The naming process, Linnaeus admitted, was tricky. Arguments raged about what constituted a species: organisms that can reproduce with each other? What is to be done with organisms that cannot reproduce, such as mules? "The first step in wisdom," wrote Linnaeus, "is to know the things themselves; this notion consists in having a sure idea of the objects; objects are distinguished and known by classifying them methodically and giving them appropriate names . . . classification and name-giving will be the foundation of our science." To a great extent he was right. Without question his system went a long way toward bringing method to the study of living things. With the publication of *Systema naturae,* Linnaeus became instantly famous. At last for many it seemed as if the logjam of classification had been broken by the Swedish naturalist. Linnaeus became a national hero, the Prince of Botanists, as many called him at the time.

Unlike many other scientific revolutions occurring during the 17th and 18th centuries, Linnaeus's great breakthrough had the misleading appearance of one without ideological violence. Unlike Copernicus and Galileo he did not seem to be upsetting the solar system or threatening established religious thought. On the contrary, it seemed he was simply following in the footsteps of Adam, giving names to the creatures of God. He had given temporal order without disrupting religious order. The Great Chain of Being remained intact. His studies and classifying had convinced him that according to God's plan, the unchangeability of the species was the rule of nature. Each creature, with its secure place in the chain, had been personally designed by the creator. While there is some evidence that later in his life Linnaeus may have begun to

Linnaeus wore Lapp apparel even after returning home. *(Courtesy of the National Library of Medicine)*

alter some of his views on new species slightly, he intended this, his most famous and influential work, to strongly support the traditional view of the fixity of the species and God's unique role in the creation.

"As there are no new species," he wrote, "(1): as like always gives birth to like (2): as one in each species was at the beginning of the progeny (3): it is necessary to attribute this progenitorial unity to some omnipotent and omniscient Being, namely *God*, whose work is called *creation*. This is confirmed by the mechanism, the laws, principles, constitutions, and sensations in every living individual."

Although he had declined to follow his father's footsteps into the ministry, his work, he believed, had allowed him to trace a more important path, one identified, as he wrote later, with "the very footprints of the creator." Always a complex individual of many contradictions, Linnaeus never abandoned either his immodesty or his piety.

So, for most, Linnaeus's new system came like an intellectual miracle. Out of the blue from an impoverished university in Sweden had arrived at last a way to come to grips with the long-standing problem of classification. Linnaeus had brought order and method to the identification of the tremendous diversity of life. Almost immediately, too, his system gave rise to a tremendous boom in worldwide specimen collection—with Linnaeus himself directing many eager students to travel the world in search of new finds. It was dangerous work; some estimates claim that one out of every three of Linnaeus's student emissaries died in their search. But no longer would new and mysterious specimens be collected only to be tucked away and forgotten in back rooms or curiosity museums. Now every plant or animal could be labeled or "identified," and each new discovery could find its rightful niche to yield new and useful knowledge in the quickly expanding map of nature. The numbers, thanks to voyages like Captain James Cook's, swelled quickly. Linnaeus knew and gave scientific names to 4,200 species of animals and 7,700 plants. Today the system has been gradually expanded to include 350,000 plants and more than a million animals.

Linnaeus's system was a heady achievement for a largely self-taught naturalist. On his return to Sweden in 1738, he entered medical practice and was appointed to a chair of medicine in 1741. A year later he moved into the chair of botany at Uppsala. In 1761 Linnaeus, the son of a poor Swedish minister, was appointed a member of the Swedish House of Nobles and given the right to go by the name Carl von Linné. Dying in 1778, he remained to the end a legend and a revered figure in his native land.

But not everyone agreed with Linnaeus's work. There were evident flaws and weaknesses, and many scientists and philosophers in the intellectually critical and skeptical 18th century were uneasy with its inconsistencies. Some of those critics began to set in motion a movement that would result, in the following century, in a revolution in biology that would be more disturbing for many even than the great Copernican revolution of the 17th century: the theory of evolution.

Carolus Linnaeus always fought against any idea of evolution—preliminary rumblings of the idea had already begun to be heard. All species, he believed, had been created separately in the beginning and no new ones, he was sure, had ever formed after the creation. Nor had any ever become extinct.

Linnaeus's work was changed slightly by those who followed him, among them Georges Cuvier, who changed some of the details to make the system of nomenclature a more natural one emphasizing relationships. Although neither Cuvier nor Linnaeus intended it, the system of classification formulated by the rigidly conservative Swedish botanist ended up leading relentlessly toward Charles Darwin and his theory of evolution in the following century.

7

Buffon and Diversity in Nature

AMONG THOSE WHO WERE SKEPTICAL about Linnaeus and his new classification system, Georges-Louis Leclerc, comte de Buffon (1707–88), was the most critical and the most influential. Born in France in the same year as Linnaeus, Buffon was in many ways Linnaeus's exact opposite. Whereas Linnaeus was born poor and struggled for money most of his life, Buffon was raised by wealthy and well-educated parents. Whereas Linnaeus was pious (his critics often said that he wrote as if he had been present at the creation), Buffon was skeptical. Whereas Linnaeus was methodical and restrained, Buffon was intuitive and speculative. Linnaeus's enemies called him stuffy, rigid, and self-righteous. Buffon's enemies called him a dandy and a playboy.

There were more basic differences, though, between the two men than social position and personality. The world for Linnaeus was the magnificent and perfect work of God. His own "modest role" in this perfect work, Linnaeus believed not too modestly, was to carry on the work of Adam—to assign identity and give names and by doing so to help us understand the wonderful, underlying order and purpose of God's universe.

Buffon's world was a world governed not by divine order and purpose but by "a system of laws, elements, and forces," a Newtonian world functioning within the laws of nature, whose processes were ends in themselves rather than a part of divine purpose or plan. A world, as Newton saw it, of motion and continuity.

Like his contemporary, Voltaire, Buffon had spent some time in England, in his case driven there by a youthful indiscretion that

Buffon spent his summers reading, studying nature, and writing at Montbard, his estate near Dijon. *(Figuier,* Vies des savants, *1870)*

resulted in a duel and temporary exile. Also like Voltaire he was quickly attracted to the beautiful logic and impressive successes of the Newtonians. To get a better hold on the English language, he translated one of Newton's works on calculus into French, and pored over English books, first on physics, his earlier interest, and then on botany. By the time he returned home to France, he had picked up not only Newtonian ideas and ideals but also English mannerisms and style.

Buffon was determined to offer the world his own comprehensive view of the universe. It was a big ambition for the formerly pampered playboy. Fortunately his work was recognized by 1739 by the French Academy of Sciences, to which he was elected an associate, and at the age of 32 he was appointed director of the royal garden, the Jardin du Roi (now the Jardin des Plantes). In this position he was able to amass an impressive collection of specimens and make the garden into a fine research center.

An Encyclopedia of Natural History

The Jardin du Roi provided grist for Buffon's intellectual mill, and he was gifted not only with intelligence and a well-honed writing style but also with enough self-knowledge to know that he needed more discipline. He spent winters in Paris, but summers he spent at his estate, Montbard, near Dijon, where he set up a Spartan regime beginning at six every morning. Knowing his own tendency to sleep in, he awarded his trusted valet extra money for successfully getting him out of bed, and he interrupted his work only twice a day to have his hair dressed and powdered. It was a discipline he maintained for 50 years. Thomas Jefferson, who was invited to dine at Montbard when he was American ambassador to France, recalled,

> It was Buffon's practice to remain in his study till dinner time, and receive no visitors under any pretense; but his house was open and his grounds, and a servant showed them very civilly, and invited all strangers and friends to remain to dine. We saw Buffon in the garden, but carefully avoided him; but we dined with him, and he proved himself then, as he always did, a man of extraordinary powers in conversation.

Buffon began writing his encyclopedic *Histoire naturelle* (*Natural History*) in 1745. The first three volumes were published in 1749 and immediately met with great success. Although he had originally planned to take only a few years and fill up just a couple of volumes, it was a project that occupied the rest of his long life and eventually filled 36 books (with the help of others) published during his lifetime, plus eight more published after his death.

Despite his tremendous discipline when it came to his writing, however, Buffon was not a very disciplined scientist. Although he was enamored of the Newtonian revolution, he was not really inclined to the kind of tough-minded observation, experimentation, and mathematical analysis that was required to perform well in the scientific arena. But what Buffon tried to accomplish was a kind of overview of the universe in which he would peek into all of its nooks and crannies and, using Newtonian ideas and the new mechanistic viewpoint, offer his own speculations on what it all was and how it all came to be.

Despite its modernity this exciting endeavor harked back in many ways to the ancients, who, Buffon pointed out, were ". . . great men and were not limited to a single field of study. They had lofty minds, wide and profound knowledge, and broad views." As if foreseeing criticism—and perhaps taking a stab at the detail-oriented

Linnaeus—he continued, ". . . If, at first glance, they seem to us to lack exactitude in certain details, it is easy to see, on reading them with reflection, they did not believe that little things merit as much attention as we have recently given them."

Needless to say, with Buffon's thinking and writing stretched out over more than 40 volumes and nearly 50 years, today's readers can find many loose ends, contradictions, errors, and instances of sloppy thinking in his momentous work. This said, then, it is important to recognize that his *Natural History*, in its time, was tremendously exciting and influential. Its volumes stimulated other, more disciplined thinkers to grab hold of some of Buffon's provocative and speculative ideas and focus their own more exacting researches.

In his first volume Buffon immediately established his differences with the Linnaean system, which he scorned as dry-as-dust compartmentalization, and with all "artificial" systems in general. "The error," he argued, "consists in failure to understand nature's processes, which always take place by graduations. . . . It is possible to descend by almost insensible degrees from the most perfect creature to the most formless matter . . . there will be found a great number of intermediate species, and of objects belonging half to one class and half to

While in charge of the Jardin du Roi, Buffon greatly expanded the garden's collection of rare and unusual plant specimens, making the place a favorite attraction for foreign dignitaries and other visitors. (*Figuier,* Vies des savants, *1870*)

another. Objects of this sort, to which it is impossible to assign a place, necessarily render vain the attempt to a universal system."

What, then, was Buffon proposing? Here the going gets tricky, since his ideas, always speculative, were in constant development and were spread out over many years and many books. His starting point was his belief that all classification systems were simply convenient products of the human mind and that nature itself was not made up of such discontinuous divisions as classes, orders, genera, or species. No matter how helpful (or harmful) such categories might be to students of nature, they were purely artificial and arbitrary. Nature, said Buffon, is composed of individual organisms that show very small and continuous gradations from one to the other. His ideas about classification apparently changed, though, over the years. In 1749, when his publications first began, he was strongly skeptical that any classification system was possible for the diverse world of living things. By 1755 he admitted that there were related species. Species, though, he argued, were "nature's only objective and fundamental realities." All other divisions remained artificial and misleading.

If he had stopped here, we would probably know Buffon today only as a mildly interesting footnote to 18th-century science history. But unlike those natural historians he scorned for writing books "filled with numerous and dry nomenclature" and "wearisome and unnatural methods," Buffon aimed to throw a wider net, to represent a lively and evocative picture of nature as a whole, to offer a wide-ranging and general history of the Earth as a home to living creatures—a magnificent machine in motion. In fact motion was the clue. For Buffon was beginning to believe that perhaps life itself was a part of the grand movement—that, like the Earth and the physical universe that was its home, life, too, was not static but evolutionary.

The Internal Mold

As described in chapter 3, Buffon had some rather amazing ideas about the longevity of the Earth's history, even though he usually tried to stay out of trouble with the church authorities, who disapproved of claims that the Earth might be older than the 6,000 years suggested by the Bible.

Life, though, was what interested Buffon the most, and once he set the stage for it by his description of the history of the Earth, he began pursuing his most seminal and interesting ideas about the development of life forms on Earth. Although the development of those ideas, spread out over many books and many years, was often erratic and sometimes contradictory, the essence of those ideas suggested the beginning of a major intellectual shift, one that would move beyond the static view of life and the intellectual bonds of the Great Chain of Being and set the stage for the great work of Charles Darwin in the 19th century.

Buffon began his speculations about life and its developments with one strong belief in mind: that life, like the universe, could only be explained and properly understood if the explanation could be done in strictly mechanistic—that is to say, Newtonian—terms. Buffon looked for physical explanations and cause-and-effect relationships. With his work on gravity, Newton had shown that such physical relationships were not always obvious. Objects did not have to be touching each other to affect each other. They did not even have to be close: Consider the effect of the Sun and the Moon on the Earth. In the life sciences, Buffon believed, this same premise could be followed.

Buffon was not averse to fudging his speculations occasionally when he ran into a dead end. He began with the long-standing problem of the embryo (which will be discussed in chapter 8, on biological reproduction, or *generation*, as it was called in the 18th century). Buffon adopted the theory, held by some, that the embryo was formed from a mixture of male and female semen in the womb. (Though it sounds strange today, the idea of female semen was common at the time.) Depending on the stage of his thinking, he theorized that the semen was made up of "organic particles" derived either from food or from the atmosphere, which was full of minute living particles. Once collected into sperm, he explained, the particles then arranged themselves into the complex structure of the embryo. How, though, do the particles "know" to form one particular species rather than another?

Here Buffon attempted, not too successfully, to put a new spin on an old idea, Plato's eternal "essences," the idea that ideal forms exist outside space and time, independent of particular manifestations. Each species, Buffon suggested, was associated with an "internal mold," which somehow directed the particles into their proper place. (What this "mold" was, how it came to be, and how it actually manipulated the particles into place, Buffon never satisfactorily explained.) As products of this internal mold, the species were "fixed." Each species was the definite and specific product of a particular mold, which had existed throughout the universe for that species since the beginning of time. The mold determined all the details of an organism, shaping disorganized organic particles into a living animal or plant having specific characteristics. Buffon even thought that these pre-existing molds would produce the same species on another planet, exactly the same as on Earth, if the correct temperature and other environmental requirements developed (a radical idea for the time). In his "internal mold" hypothesis, Buffon differed from other, even more radical materialists who maintained that the origin of all life began as a result of spontaneous generation—at random, governed entirely by circumstances.

But Buffon also recognized, despite his attachment to this concept of immutability, that species did seem to change. During the course of his observations, he noticed, for example, the existence of rudimentary organs that were imperfectly formed and had no apparent purpose. "The pig," he wrote, "does not appear to have formed upon the original special and perfect plan, since it is a compound of other animals: it has evidently useless parts, or rather parts of which it cannot make any use, toes all of the bones of which are perfectly formed and which nevertheless are of no service to it." these "useless parts" seemed to suggest the existence of imperfections in the species. If every species was perfectly formed from the beginning of time and had never changed since then, why would these imperfections exist now? This, he explained, was a process he called "degeneration," in response to the environment. But Buffon also believed that a species would revert back to its original form once the environmental influences that caused the degeneration were removed. Here again he differed from later theories of evolution, which would see these changes as part of a continuing flow of change, not as temporary or reversible. (Buffon's ideas, by the way, caused a stir even in far-off America, prompting Thomas Jefferson to send him the skin of a large American panther to refute Buffon's claim that New World animals had degenerated in size.)

Buffon's Legacy

Buffon was provocative, his writing was elegant, and his influence as a popularizer of science was broad, and he had a considerable impact, not only on young zoologists of his day but also on the populace as a whole. Most of his work consisted of superbly written monographs on individual mammal species notable both for their scientific and their

Buffon's clear descriptions and voluminous writings, including his contributions to the *Encyclopédie,* provide a rich legacy, even though his philosophical position on issues is often difficult to discern. *(Courtesy of the National Library of Medicine)*

literary value. While many of his ideas shot wide of the mark, he stimulated thinking with his broad brush strokes where Linnaeus had plunged deep into the details. He resisted the idea of evolution of the species, steadfastly denying any such possibility; yet the facts he assembled seemed to point away from the doctrine of "fixed species" he supported. In fact Charles Darwin considered Buffon to be "the first author who in modern times had treated [the origin of species] in a scientific spirit."

Buffon's double talk may have been an attempt to avoid trouble with the church authorities; many of his more radical contemporaries thought he equivocated too much. Or perhaps his work just reflected his own changes in opinion over the long period of time during which he wrote his books. In any case he did not escape the church's ire entirely. On June 15, 1751, Buffon was called before the Faculty of Theology at the Sorbonne and instructed to withdraw certain parts of *Natural History,* which, according to his critics, contradicted dogma. Specifically the authorities cited those portions concerning the age of the Earth, the birth of the planets from the Sun, and his contention that truth can only be arrived at through science. Buffon promised to subdue the offending heresies and to tone down his writing in the future. But he continued to write provocatively, if cautiously. Buffon died in 1788. More because he was part of the aristocracy than because of his controversial ideas, revolutionaries vandalized Buffon's grave and the monument that had been raised to him. But his spirit inspired several great natural historians of his time, including Jean-Baptiste de Monet de Lamarck and Georges Cuvier, both of whom will be discussed in chapter 9.

8

The Animal Machine

Physiology, Reproduction, and Embryology

BUFFON, OF COURSE WAS NOT alone in attracting accusations of heresy. No one in the 18th century exemplified the materialist doctrine of the post-Newtonian era more than Julien Offroy de La Mettrie, author of *L'Homme machine* (Man, the machine), a little book published in 1748. And probably no one more completely outraged the church authorities (except, perhaps, Voltaire).

La Mettrie had a long history of getting in trouble with authorities. Early in his career he had translated into French the works of Hermann Boerhaave, a widely respected Dutch teacher and writer in medicine and chemistry, and incurred the wrath of the medical faculty at the University of Paris (which was so conservative that its members still had not accepted the works of Vesalius and Harvey from the 16th and 17th centuries). An incorrigible renegade, La Mettrie continued to get himself into trouble by publishing satirical pamphlets about the faculty and numerous heretical books. Though he himself was a priest, La Mettrie seemed to have no problem with setting forth materialist ideas that ran counter to religious dogma.

L'Homme machine, La Mettrie's most famous work, was published in Leiden (in the Netherlands, which was more liberal than France), probably in hopes of slipping it by the conservative French church authorities. In it he described man as a machine governed completely by physical and chemical agents. It was a radical idea,

Here Bernard de Jussieu, professor of botany at the Jardin du Roi, carries a cedar of Lebanon he is importing to France. Exploratory voyages such as Captain James Cook's worldwide expeditions and Linnaeus's journey to Lapland greatly increased scientists' awareness of the vast diversity of living things in other parts of the world. The resulting influx of specimens contributed to new understanding of the processes and nature of life. *(Figuier,* Vies des savants, *1870)*

the ultimate application of the Newtonian revolution to humanity itself. He also denied the dualism established by Descartes, which emphasized a dichotomy, or division, between mind, or soul, and body. A human being, La Mettrie maintained, can be seen as just another animal, a sort of "talking monkey." With his book La Mettrie set the stage like no one before him for modern biology, by looking at humans as not essentially different from animals.

Inspired by La Mettrie—who was more a polemicist and philosopher than a scientist—and the work of William Harvey before him, 18th-century scientists set about systematically exploring the machinery of all biological organisms. In the process three main areas of thrust emerged in the battle for understanding: the effort to understand the physiological mechanisms (including digestion and respiration) that make living organisms work, the reproductive process, and embryo development.

For the post-Newtonian biologists, the Body Machine was the idea of the age. Harvey had shown with his study of circulation that blood coursed through arteries and veins like water through pipes, controlled by valves and pumped by the heart. No one wanted to accept the idea that the analogy of body and machine could only go so far.

What Makes Animals Tick?

ALBRECHT VON HALLER

One of the most outstanding biologists of the 18th century, Albrecht von Haller was born in Bern, Switzerland, in 1708. Along with his many students (he was also one of the great teachers of the century), he explored the form and function of one organ after the other, establishing anatomy as an experimental science, and also applying dynamic principles to the study of physiology.

Haller was an exacting and painstaking experimentalist, whose quest to observe, note, and know was so great that, even on his deathbed, he remained a scientist to his last breath. In his last moments, on December 12, 1777, surrounded by physicians and friends, he placed a finger on his wrist, felt the thready pulse wane and falter, and reported dispassionately, "The artery no longer beats."

With equal determination, during his lifetime Haller explored the irritability of muscle and the sensibility of nerves, made important contributions to the physiology of the circulation, including circulation time and the automatic action of the heart, and gave the first solid discussion of respiration.

His *Elementa Physiologiae Corporis Humani* (*Elements of Physiology*, 1757–66) was known for being the last word of the century on the subject. The great 19th-century physiologist François Magendi once complained that whenever he thought he had conceived a new experiment, he would find it already described in detail by Haller in the *Elements of Physiology*. Haller systematically extended the knowledge of anatomy, linked it to physiology by experiment, and applied dynamic principles to physiological problems.

In vivisection experiments (done on living organisms), he demonstrated his painstaking methodology, a consistent, step-by-step approach to understanding function and process. He defined as "irritable" those parts that contracted when touched, and as "sensible" those parts that conveyed a message to the brain when stimulated. He tried various stimuli—pricking, pinching, and certain chemicals. He tested tendons, bones, cerebral membrane, liver,

Albrecht von Haller is considered one of the greatest modern physiologists. *(Courtesy of the National Library of Medicine)*

spleen, and kidney, all of which he found insensitive. He also found that irritability in muscles is caused by stimulation of nerves. For example, he could cause the diaphragm to contract by irritating several nerves in the area. So he explored the nature of contractile forces that occur spontaneously in muscle tissue of living animals or those that have just died.

His approach was always analytical, objective, and forward moving on the basis of data discovered. "As the nature of the brain and of the nerves is one and the same," he wrote regarding his study of the brain and nervous system, "so are these alike in function. In treating them we will so far as possible make use of our experiments, nor will we at first at least go beyond the testimony of our senses."

By experiments he found that only nerves serve as instruments of sensation and therefore only those parts of the body connected to the nervous system experience sensation.

Haller's work was unflagging and thorough, with experimental claims always substantiated by evidence. He could, of course, throw his weight behind a misleading theory, as will be explained later in this chapter, but he epitomized the biological experimenter of his time, and, overall, his greatest contribution was to the spirit and method of physiological research. Though he is comparatively unknown today, his influence throughout Europe in his time and his general intellectual activity is said to be equaled only by Voltaire's.

RENÉ-ANTOINE RÉAUMUR

Considered one of the founders of entomology, René-Antoine Réaumur (1683–1757) wrote a six-volume compendium on the life cycles and behavior of insects. His observations of living insects were so superb that they served to set the stage for *L'Histoire naturelle* by

René-Antoine Réaumur closely studied the behavior of insects and bugs, such as caterpillars and moths. *(Figuier,* Vies des savants, *1870)*

Lazzaro Sallanzani, one of the greatest of all life sciences experimenters, performing an experiment on digestion in birds (*Figuier,* Vies des savants, *1870)*

Buffon, his contemporary and rival. (In fact Réaumur may have been behind the attack on Buffon made by the theological faculty of the Sorbonne.)

In Réaumur's work he also emphasized the larger groupings of insects, rather than getting into tedious description of species, thereby setting the stage for Cuvier and his modifications to Linnaeus's system of classification (see chapter 9). Réaumur also invented a thermometric scale and a type of porcelain, and his researchers helped establish the French tin-plate industry, as well as contributing greatly to steel making in France. But in biology his rare commitment to understanding the process of digestion is perhaps his greatest claim to fame.

He had a pet hawk of a type that vomits up indigestible foods, and Réaumur trained his pet to swallow small open-ended metal tubes containing sponges. When these tubes, predictably, came back up, he examined the sponges and found that, as the bird had attempted to digest them, they were soaked with gastric juice. Réaumur then took the gastric juice and showed that the juice, when applied to meat, tended to soften it. "When I put some of the juice from the buzzard's stomach on my tongue," he wrote, "it tasted salt rather than bitter, although the bones . . . on which the fluid had acted, had not a salt but a bitter taste." He also found that when he placed bits of meat in the tubes, they came back up partly digested— but not, as some theorists had suggested, either ground up or putrefied (rotted).

LAZZARO SPALLANZANI

Lazzaro Spallanzani (1729–99) continued Réaumur's experiments, recognizing that when testing the effectiveness of gastric juices on meat, the temperature should be the same as the body temperature of the animal the juice came from. Spallanzani tried the same process with other birds, including a crow, by using string to pull the partially digested material back up. He found that after seven hours most foods were completely dissolved by the juices.

Not content with these results, though, Spallanzani went a step further, experimenting on himself. Though afraid he might choke and die (as in fact Réaumur's pet hawk had), he swallowed a small linen bag containing a few grains of chewed bread. When the bag emerged from his system 23 hours later, the bread was gone,

Italian physiologist Giovanni Morgagni (1682–1771) examined the anatomy of diseased, instead of healthy, tissue—providing new insights into the causes and progress of disease from an anatomical viewpoint. From his work in 640 postmortem dissections, the science of pathology evolved, of which he is considered the founder. *(Courtesy of Parke-Davis Division of Warner-Lambert Company)*

although the bag was still in good shape. He later tried swallowing wooden spheres and open-ended metal tubes containing food, with the ends covered with gauze, but he gagged on them. His scientific curiosity, he had found, had run up against its limits on this particular subject.

Lavoisier Cracks the Respiration Problem

So much of progress in science depends on all the previous hurdles having been jumped so that when a person with a certain perspective, background, and aptitude comes along, he or she has a clear track ahead. Antoine Lavoisier, who also did so much in other areas of chemistry, had the superb luck to come to the problem of respiration with all the necessary hurdles behind him: Harvey had explained the circulation of the blood; an understanding of the movements involved in respiration had been achieved; the microanatomy of the lungs had been done by Malpighi; and the chemistry of gases, thanks in part to his own efforts, was now far more in hand than ever before. By the end of the century, successful isolation and characterization of the gases had produced a revolution in chemistry (see chapter 4), and now, at last, respiration began to fall into place.

By 1777 Lavoisier had published a paper entitled "Experiments on the Respiration of Animals and on the Changes Which the Air Undergoes in Passing through the Lungs." Now that he understood the nature of the gases involved—"eminently respirable" air (oxygen) and "fixed air" (carbon dioxide)—Lavoisier could explain that respiration was a slow combustion or oxidation. Although his English colleague Joseph Priestley had missed the point, Lavoisier grasped that respiration used oxygen and released carbon dioxide. He collaborated with Pierre-Simon Laplace (see chapter 2) to design an experimental device that could provide a quantitative measurement of the production of animal heat, in order to investigate the physiochemical basis of respiration. Using the ice-calorimeter they developed, they could compare respiration and combustion quantitatively, with exciting results. No longer was the comparison of respiration and combustion just a nice metaphor. Lavoisier was now able to conclude in his "Memoir on Heat" that "the heat released in the conversion of pure air to fixed air by respiration is the principal cause of the maintenance of animal heat."

How Do Organisms Reproduce?

One of the toughest problems facing those interested in natural history was the question about how animals came to have offspring. First of all the ovum (or egg) in the mammal was not even discovered until 1828, and no one observed the union of an egg nucleus and a sperm until the end of the 19th century. Those key discoveries required techniques and equipment not available to 18th-century scientists. As a result many 18th-century ideas were really guesses, and they had a lot of them—sometimes based on evidence, sometimes based on intuition, and sometimes based on their favorite worldview. Some naturalists thought that the egg (for example, in chickens or frogs) had nothing to do with fertilization and the growth of the embryo. Many others either denied the existence of

Edward Jenner:
Vanquishing Smallpox

While Edward Jenner (1749–1823) was still a young medical apprentice, he began thinking about a remark he had heard from a country dairymaid. The girl argued that she never had to worry about contracting smallpox since she had already once contracted cowpox. Cowpox was an extremely mild disease that was quite common and was transferred from the udder of a cow to the hands of its milker, resulting in pustular eruptions similar to (but much less serious than) smallpox. The fact that contracting cowpox led to immunity to smallpox was common knowledge in the rural Gloucestershire area where Jenner practiced as a country doctor.

It was already widely known that if a person survived a mild form of smallpox, he or she was immune from further infection, and in fact some

Edward Jenner administering a smallpox vaccination *(Courtesy of Parke-Davis Division of Warner-Lambert Company)*

physicians were already inoculating a few wealthy patients against a mild form of the disease to protect them from the great smallpox epidemics that swept in waves across 18th-century Europe. The inoculation was expensive and the injections were almost as dangerous as the disease itself. The procedure sometimes proved fatal, and it usually left the patient covered with ugly scars.

Jenner spent nearly 20 years studying the problem while keeping careful notes on cowpox and smallpox patients. Finally, in May 1796, he ran his experiment. Using the cowpox pus from the hand of an infected dairymaid, he "vaccinated" an eight-year-old boy named James Phipps. The boy contracted a mild case of cowpox, as Jenner had expected, but quickly recovered, also as Jenner had hoped. The next step came two months later when Jenner inoculated the boy with what should have been a lethal dose of smallpox. It was a dangerous and controversial experiment, but the boy remained healthy and showed no signs of being infected with the deadly disease. Jenner repeated his test a few months later, again injecting young Phipps with yet another strong dose of the smallpox serum. Again the boy remained healthy.

Jenner concluded that the cowpox virus was similar enough to the smallpox that the body could build a resistance to both at the same time, but the cowpox disease was so mild that being inoculated with it caused only minor discomfort.

Coining the word *vaccination* from the Latin word for "cowpox" (*vaccinia* from the Latin for "cow": *vacca*), Jenner published his findings. Although there was skepticism and some resistance at first, vaccination was completely accepted in England by 1800 and was soon being adopted by the rest of the world. At one point Jenner himself was vaccinating more than 300 poor people a day in the garden of his country home. By 1800 an estimated 100,000 persons had received the new immunization, and many countries soon made vaccinations mandatory, after which the number of cases of smallpox dropped dramatically.

Although it was later discovered that the vaccination against smallpox did not last for a lifetime but had to be "refreshed" or "boosted" later, Jenner's treatment not only helped to rid the world of a dread disease but established the science of immunization and opened the door to research later done by Pasteur, Koch, and others looking for cures and immunizations against other diseases.

sperm or classified them as parasites, useless if not harmful to the reproduction process. Many, including Linnaeus, thought that external fertilization never occurred; Linnaeus flatly asserted, "Never, in any living body, does fecundation or impregnation of eggs take place outside the body of the mother." Some, though not all, of these questions were addressed by the excellent experimental work done by Lazzaro Spallanzani.

Spallanzani's passion for science was probably encouraged by his cousin Laura Bassi (1711–78), who held a chair in mathematics at the University of Bologna, a rare distinction for a woman in her time. (See sidebar in chapter 1.) Spallanzani's interests ranged wide, from geology (he led an expedition to Mt. Etna during its eruption) to physiology to physics (he held the chair of physics and mathematics at the University of Reggio) to Greek to philosophy (both of which he taught). But, despite his divergent interests, Spallanzani is considered

The Spontaneous Generation Controversy in the 18th Century

The idea that some organisms may originate spontaneously from inorganic matter has come and gone many times—and, at a molecular level, has played an important part in several widely respected 20th-century theories of the origin of life.

In the 17th century Francesco Redi put to rest the idea, fostered by the Greek thinker Aristotle, that organisms (such as maggots, tapeworms, or insects) could suddenly spring from slime or a piece of aging meat or rotting flesh or excreta. But, with the discovery of microscopic organisms in the 17th century, the question of spontaneous generation rose again (although their discoverer, Anthoni van Leeuwenhock, thought that they came from parents like themselves).

In the 18th century Buffon threw his rather significant weight behind the idea of spontaneous generation. A friend of his, English microscopist John Needham (1713–81), collaborated with him on a series of experiments in 1748 that seemed conclusive. Needham boiled mutton broth and sealed it in glass containers. A few days later, when he opened the containers, he found numerous microorganisms present. His conclusion: that microorganisms had been produced from nonliving matter. "There is a vegetato be one of the greatest of all experimenters. Through his carefully controlled experiments he overcame—at least temporarily—the age-old belief in spontaneous generation. He also found time to perform some very interesting experiments regarding reproduction.

One idea that had been set forth by several prominent 17th-century scientists, including Harvey and Fabricius, was that the active agent for fertilization was contained in the semen but was not part of it. In fact they thought it was nonmaterial, an invisible power, like magnetic power, and they called it *aura seminalis*. Working with frogs, Spallanzani was able to prove that this idea of the aura seminalis was incorrect. He did experiments in which the female was killed while the eggs were being emitted. Eggs that were normally emitted and came in contact with semen developed as usual. Those that were taken from the body of the female by dissection, that had never come in contact with the semen (though presumably nearby

tive Force in every microscopical Point of Matter," he deduced, "and every visible Filament of which the whole animal or vegetable Texture consists . . ." In line with suggestions made by mathematician-philosopher Gottfried Wilhelm Leibniz (1646–1716) of the existence of "monads" or living molecules, Needham thought that animals and plants decomposed, when they died, to "a kind of universal *Semen*," a "Source of all," from which new living matter arises again and again.

But 20 years later Lazzaro Spallanzani repeated the experiment, this time using more scientific controls. He boiled different flasks for different lengths of time and discovered that some types of microbes were more resistant to heat than others. Some died after slight heating, but others survived boiling for as long as an hour. In Needham's experiment, Spallanzani pointed out, some spores present in the original mutton broth had survived the short boiling period used.

Spallanzani's experiments certainly proved the necessity of thorough sterilizing techniques, and, for the moment, they laid to rest the idea of spontaneous generation. But in 1810 the French chemist Joseph Louis Gay-Lussac argued that Spallanzani's sterile vessels had lacked oxygen—which would be necessary for spontaneously generated life. This point called the conclusiveness of Spallanzani's experiments into question and left the question of spontaneous generation up in the air once again.

enough to have been exposed, theoretically, to any aura the semen might have) did not develop.

While these results looked good, Spallanzani decided to go one step further. He fashioned pairs of tight-fitting taffeta pants for the male frogs in the next experiment. Despite the strange costume the frogs tried to mate as usual. But this time no seminal fluid could reach the female or her eggs. The semen, and all it contained, was retained inside the pants, and though the female discharged many eggs, none of them developed. But when Spallanzani painted some of them with some of the fluid retained in the taffeta pants: Voilà! The eggs that were painted developed normally. Spallanzani also collected semen directly from the male's seminal vesicles and carefully applied them to eggs. Those eggs that were treated in this way developed into tadpoles. One of the techniques of sound scientific experimentation involves keeping "controls" to make sure that the outcome being observed would not happen even if the experimenter had done nothing. So Spallanzani also included eggs in this experiment that were not treated—and these disintegrated. (If they had developed into tadpoles, too, he would have had to ask himself a lot of questions about the design of the experiment, about his procedures, and about his basic assumptions. He would also have had to refigure his conclusions—or, more likely, reserve making any conclusions until he could run the experiment again.)

Spallanzani had come upon a method of artificial insemination. In 1779 he cinched the case when he successfully used a similar process on a female dog. Although he certainly was not the first to perform artificial insemination successfully (Arabian horse breeders have been doing it for centuries), Spallanzani was the first to perform the experiment scientifically, with careful controls and documentation of results.

He created quite a stir in the scientific community, to say the least, and in 1781 the Swiss naturalist Charles Bonnet (1720–93) wrote to him, predicting with some clarity, "I do not know, but one day what you have discovered may be applied in the human species to ends we little think and with no light consequences."

But the question still remained which portion of the semen actually caused impregnation. So Bonnet suggested another experiment to Spallanzani, leading to another series of cliffhangers. Spallanzani placed a carefully measured quantity of semen on a watch glass. Then, using a small amount of gluten, a natural glue, he attached

26 eggs to another watch glass, turned it upside down, and placed it over the watch glass containing the semen. The eggs were moist, and some of the semen apparently disappeared (presumably evaporated), but the eggs did not actually come in contact with the semen. When placed in water, these eggs did not develop. But when he painted the semen onto other eggs, they did develop, demonstrating that the semen was still potent. Once and for all the aura seminalis was crossed off the list of suspects. From this Spallanzani concluded that "fecundation [or fertilization] in the fetid toad is not the effect of the aura seminalis, but of the sensible [perceivable with senses] part of the seed."

Bonnet suggested testing whether other influences—blood, blood extracts, electricity, vinegar, wine, urine, lemon and lime juices, oils, and more—might have interesting results. Spallanzani followed up on the suggestions, but none of these influences caused any development whatever. He tried to test how virile the semen was—what could take its ability to impregnate away—and he discovered several things that did not work, including dilution, exposure to a vacuum, cold, and oil. However, semen did not fare well when exposed to heat, evaporation, or wine, or when passed through a filter paper.

This last piece of information gave Spallanzani an idea for another experiment, in which he filtered the semen. The result was a thin liquid that had no power to fertilize eggs, and, in the filter paper, a thick, gummy residue remained. When Spallanzani tried painting this residue on the eggs, again the eggs developed. But for some reason Spallanzani ignored the significance of this important detail, coming to the conclusion that it was not the sperm left in the filter paper but the small portion of seminal fluid that was left behind that fertilized the eggs. So Spallanzani should have concluded correctly from his experiment that it is the sperm, not the fluid around the sperm, that does the deed. But for some reason that perhaps no one will ever understand, he did not reach this conclusion. He had some previous experimental results that seemed to cloud the issue—seminal fluid that he thought was free of sperm that fertilized, seminal fluid that contained sperm apparently killed by exposure or rune or vinegar that had worked. Or maybe he was thrown off course by his belief that sperm were parasites passed from generation to generation through intercourse, a sort of universal venereal disease.

Meanwhile the question of how an animal develops once an egg is fertilized was still very much up in the air.

Wolff Challenges Preformation

"The ovary of an ancestress," Haller once wrote, "will contain not only her daughter, but also her granddaughter, her great-grand-daughter, and her great-great-grand-daughter, and if it is once proved that an ovary can contain many generations, there is no absurdity in saying that it contains them all." Known as preformation this idea had been around a long time—although, depending on which theory of reproduction one subscribed to, the "homunculus," as this tiny preformed human was called, might be located either in the ovum or in the sperm. Imaginative microscopists had even drawn tiny little men they thought they had seen huddled inside the confines of a single sperm cell.

But Caspar Friedrich Wolff (1734–94) brought a new approach to the analysis of embryo development and differentiation. In 1759

A typical microscope of the 1700s
(Courtesy of Bausch and Lomb)

he wrote a landmark dissertation entitled *Theoria generationes* (Theory of generation), in which he changed the course of the history of embryology. In it he recounted observations he had made on plants and outlined the philosophical premise that embryonic development was "epigenetic," that is, progressed through the gradual addition of parts.

Apparently unaware that most of his colleagues—including the great physiologist Albrecht von Haller—subscribed adamantly to the concept of preformation, Wolff sent his thesis to Haller (Wolff was only 26 at the time). Haller quickly rejected Wolff's thesis on religious grounds. No doubt feeling rebuffed, Wolff replied pointedly that a scientist must search for truth, without pre-judging materials on religious, not scientific grounds. For his part, though, Wolff was just setting forth a relatively unsubstantiated hypothesis; so his thesis, at this point, lacked the clout to stand up against Haller's objection.

But 18th-century biologists had come up against a dilemma. Although Haller, Spallanzani, and Bonnet all felt comfortable with the religious framework and wanted to maintain allegiance to the biblical story of creation, they wanted to think of biological reproduction in the same mechanistic terms that they used for all the other aspects of physiology on which they were all working.

Using the experimental approach to crack this case posed problems. Microscopes had not improved particularly since the days of van Leeuwenhoek. Staining techniques, which would enable biologists to differentiate various kinds of tissue and cells, had not yet developed. More progress had been made with plants because details in plants are easier to see through a microscope than unstained animal tissues. So most of Wolff's conclusions for both plants and animals were based on his microscopic examination of plants alone. There, in the seed, he saw in the primordial undifferentiated material the rudiments of leaves and parts of flowers.

Then in 1768 Wolff described new researches he had succeeded in doing on the formation of the intestine of the chick. He had found that the chick intestine developed from a simple sheet of tissue as the embryo developed. It folded along its length to form a trough and then closed to form a tube. He also discovered in higher animals that an embryonic kidney develops that then later disappears before development is complete. (In his honor the structure is now known as the Wolffian body.) In these two cases, he maintained, preformation theory could not hold up. The chick intestine could not have been preformed in the egg; he had watched it develop stage by stage. The process, he concluded, must be differentiation of simple uniform (homogeneous) tissue into more complex, heterogeneous (different) structures.

"We may conclude," Wolff wrote, "that the organs of the body have not always existed, but have been formed successively; no matter how this formation had been brought about. I do not say it has been brought about by a fortuitous combination of particles, by a kind of fermentation, through mechanical causes or through activity of the soul, *but only that is has been brought about.*"

Wolff was one of the first biologists to become a proponent of *Naturphilosophie* (nature philosophy), a German philosophy influenced by romanticism, which held that nature was permeated by a life force that infused the process of creation and reproduction.

As a subscriber to *Naturphilosophie*, he thought the process he had observed exhibited a kind of life force that worked upon homogeneous organic matter, building it up into structures. But he could go no further.

In the end, although Wolff had gone far (T. H. Huxley considered him a greatly underrated genius), he could not win the battle against the theory of preformation. For that battle scientists needed the development of cell theory to provide a framework, for understanding the sperm, egg, and embryo. Secondly biologists would have to give up their favorite 18th-century ideas—both mechanism and *Naturphilosophie*. They had to give up trying to see organisms as machines, while not giving up the hope of explaining the mechanism that makes them work. Those who fought to understand the process of embryo development, like those struggling to grapple with the great questions of evolution, would only see their battle won in the coming era of the 19th century.

9

Precursors to Modern Evolutionary Theory
Lamarck and Cuvier

THE 18TH-CENTURY STRUGGLE over "fixity of the species"—the idea that all the species remained exactly as they always were—came to a climax at the end of the century in the work of two men, Jean-Baptiste de Monet de Lamarck (who is known as Lamarck) and Georges Cuvier. The fact that they were both French probably was no accident; Paris by this time had become the center for biological studies. The city itself sat in a vast basin, a burial ground containing hundreds of thousands of shells, corals, mammals, and a great repository fossils. The two men, Lamarck and Cuvier, became arch rivals, one an expert on invertebrates (animals having no backbones), the other an expert on vertebrates (those having backbones).

Lamarck Opens the Door to Evolution

Charles Darwin once called Lamarck "the first man whose conclusions on the subject [of where species came from] excited much attention, . . ." one who "did the eminent service of arousing attention to the probability of all change in the organic, as well as in the inorganic world, being the result of law, and not of miraculous interposition." His place in science history is often overshadowed by Darwin's own enormous contribution in the following century and by the ridicule Lamarck received from his colleagues in his own time. But Lamarck

Pioneering evolutionist Jean-Baptiste de Monet, chevalier de Lamarck *(Courtesy, Burndy Library)*

was among the first to have the courage to set forth the idea that species are not fixed, but transformed from generation to generation and over time. He was a man of brilliant intuitions, although he sometimes extended his speculations too far beyond his scientific knowledge base—attempting to synthesize theories, not only about biology, but also about physics and chemistry (in which he loudly opposed Lavoisier's breakthroughs).

Born the youngest in a family of 11 children, Jean-Baptiste-Pierre-Antione de Monet (1744–1829) nonetheless acquired the family title, chevalier de Lamarck. But that was the extent of his good fortune, for no income went with the title. As a young man with no real prospects, he was sent to study with the Jesuits to become a priest (his aristocratic family recognizing no other means of self-support honorable, except a military career). But as soon as Lamarck's father died, with what meager inheritance he did acquire, he bought a horse and rode away from his future life in the clergy. At the age of 16, he joined the German army; he distinguished himself during the Seven Years' War and was promoted for bravery. But a chronic inflammation of the lymph nodes in his neck nipped that career in the bud at age 22. So, still seeking his fortune, Lamarck went to Paris, where he married several times; studied botany, medicine, and music; and worked as a bank clerk.

During this period he became a friend of the philosopher Jean-Jacques Rousseau, with whom he went on long walks, discussing nature and natural history. He found he could support himself by writing, turning out a couple of lackluster books on medicine and an annual almanac that, year after year, for 11 years provided totally unreliable weather predictions based on his own system of meteorology.

But Lamarck's career really began to take off when he went back to the interest in plant life that had first been kindled when he was stationed in the army along the Mediterranean coast. He wrote a book on French plant life (*Flore française*), which was published in 1778 and met with great success, going through several printings. It was the first field guide to be organized as a key to help readers identify species of French flowers, and it was widely used by botanists and casual hikers alike.

Aided by Buffon, who took an interest in him and hired him to tutor his son, Lamarck's career in natural history began. In 1781 he became an assistant in the botanical department of the king's natural history museum, a paid position that gave him the opportunity to travel widely, collecting botanical specimens for the museum. Then came the Revolution. The regime by which he and Buffon were employed came to an end, and the old Jardin du Roi in Paris became the new Museum of Natural History. But with the Revolution came a stroke of luck. In 1793, when the revolutionaries were casting about for someone to name to the lowly position of professor of insects, shells, and worms (what we know today as invertebrate zoology) at the museum, Lamarck was chosen—despite his lack of any real background in the subject. (At about the same time his future rival Cuvier was named to the clearly more prestigious position of professor of vertebrate zoology.) Unflappable, however, Lamarck saw his opportunity and, at the age of nearly 50, plunged into the subject, producing prodigious results, including a seven-volume *History of Invertebrates*.

Lamarck succeeded in bringing order where Linnaeus had left a sort of indiscriminate hodgepodge. Lamarck differentiated the arachnids (spiders, ticks, mites, and scorpions, all of which have eight legs) from the insects (which have only six). He established categories for crustaceans (crabs, lobsters, crayfish, and the like) and echinoderms (those with external spines, such as starfish and sea urchins). Lamarck in fact established the words *invertebrate* and *vertebrate* and coined the word *biology*.

In his best work, *Zoological Philosophy*, published in 1809, Lamarck set forth two factors that he believed were important to the evolution of the species: first, that all creatures have a fundamental tendency to evolve into higher life forms and that nature itself tends toward an increasing complexity; and second, the idea for which he is best known and most criticized, the inheritance of acquired characteristics.

Lamarck thought that life was generated spontaneously from a gelatin or mucouslike material, aided in the process by heat or electricity,

The Hunter Brothers: Tale of a Ruffian Scientist

William Hunter (1718–83) was building a reputation for himself in London as one of England's top physicians and anatomists; meanwhile, his younger brother John (1728–93) was building a different kind of reputation in Glasgow. In contrast to his serious-minded brother, John was considered a wild, heavy-drinking, and barely literate lout by everyone who knew him. He drank too much, fought too much, swore too much, and rode his horse too wildly over the Scottish countryside. His one virtue, the townspeople said, was that he could work with his hands and seemed to have a natural gift with tools in his job as a cabinetmaker.

Why in the world his brother William invited him to come to London and take a job as his assistant in his private anatomical laboratory was a mystery to everyone. Just about everyone also thought that no good would come of it for either brother.

There was no denying John's skilled hands, though, and although he did not give up his wild living, he quickly progressed from performing dissections (while his brother William lectured) to becoming the supervisor of William's laboratory. William, in fact, was so pleased with his younger brother's performance (although still disturbed by his unruly habits) that he managed to get John permission to study at the Chelsea Military Hospital. Surprisingly John breezed through with distinction, and in 1754 he studied surgery at St. George's Hospital. After a year as resident surgeon, he joined his older brother as a full partner in William's private anatomical school.

All was not smooth, though, between the brothers. John was still refusing to wear his appropriate wig and insisted upon being called "Jack." And he was not too happy when William talked him into entering Oxford. "They wanted to make an old woman out of me, trying to stuff me with Latin and Greek," he told his friends after he dropped out as soon as the first term finished.

He did manage to improve his reading and writing, although he never felt comfortable with either. He did pick up a taste for good living, including the best seats at the theater and moving in London's elite social circles. More important he quickly became known as one of London's most important researchers into the basic aspect of biology. He was also rapidly passing up his older brother, not only in research—he traced the development of the testes in the male fetus, followed the nasal and olfactory cranial nerves, and studied the formation of pus—but also in his reputation as an anatomist.

A multitalented pioneer, John Hunter is best remembered for the museum of comparative anatomy he assembled to illustrate concepts in comparative structure and function of organs. Unfortunately, many of the specimens were destroyed during World War II. *(Courtesy of Parke-Davis Division of Warner-Lambert Company)*

William's reputation was firm. His specialty was obstetrics, and, with his scientific methods, he had succeeded in greatly reducing London's mortality rate during childbirth. In many ways his had been a heroic effort, requiring a long fight to break the hold of midwifery in childbirth, a practice that had in the 17th century degenerated from a warm and caring procedure to an often careless one performed for quick profit by ill-trained practitioners.

Still William probably was not too unhappy when his younger brother, concerned about his health, decided that he needed a warmer climate and joined the military as a surgeon. With his condition improved after a stint in Portugal—where he also spent time studying animal and plant specimens—John became staff surgeon on a military expedition to Belle Isle, a small island in the Atlantic. During fighting

(continues)

(continued)

there between British and Spanish troops, he began an important study of gunshot wounds and developed his reputation as a surgeon still further.

Returning to London, John discovered that his former position at William's school had been filled, and he set up a private practice on his own. Like his older brother he also taught anatomy and surgery. Despite his continued disdain for "book learning," he was the much more scientific of the two brothers, developing and taking special care of his procedures. Dissecting and studying more than 500 species of animals, John did pioneering work in the study of the lymphatic system, demonstrated that tendons would reunite after being severed, and made major investigations in the study of blood coagulation. He also worked on problems dealing with the embryology of the chick, and his preserved works in this area include some of the most beautiful and accurate drawings ever made on the subject.

Elected a fellow of the Royal Society of London in 1767, John managed to overcome his discomfort with writing often enough to make many major and varied contributions to the literature of science. His work demonstrated his agile and curious mind, ranging from "A Treatise of the Natural History of Human Teeth" to "Directions for Preserving Animals and Parts of Animals for Anatomical Investigations" to "Observations and Reflections on Geology."

Not surprisingly, during the latter part of his life, John found himself in many heated quarrels with his brother (each claimed the other had at various times "borrowed" from his work), and their disputes continued until William's death in 1783. John died 10 years later as a result of an experiment he had begun in 1767, when he inoculated himself with the pus of a syphilitic patient. Ironically his theories about syphilis and gonorrhea (too involved to go into here) were wrong and, beside misleading the study of syphilis for half a century, led to his death in 1793.

Characteristically he studied the progression of the disease in himself until the end. Characteristically, too, he died following a heated quarrel with a colleague at a board meeting of the Royal Society. The immediate cause of his death was stated to be apoplexy, but more likely it was untreated syphilis.

and he disagreed with those who thought that great floods and other catastrophes had marked the history of the plant and animal world. Living beings, he thought, had experienced gradual changes in their environment over vast spans of time—in fact, Lamarck had a closer grasp than most of his contemporaries of the colossal length of geological time. These long-term changes in the environment, he thought, had not directly created changes in the species. But Lamarck proposed that changes in the environment affected the nervous system, which brought about changes in the entire structure of creatures: An urge, or a sense of need, within the animal somehow created changes in muscles and organs to respond to the changing demands of its surroundings. Lamarck thought that requirements of an animal's life actually shaped its organs and that these traits, when shared by male and female, were then passed on to the animal's offspring. For example, giraffes (which he believed began as antelope) stretched their legs, necks, and tongues to reach the high leaves off the trees. Each generation succeeded in stretching a little farther, passing longer and longer legs, necks, and tongues on to their offspring, until finally the giraffe as we know it today emerged. Other animal traits also evolved over time from generation to generation. Moles and blind mice, for example, cannot see because they live underground and have lost the sight of their eyes through disuse. Ducks' toes are webbed from stretching to paddle against the water. Lamarck did not say that species acquire new characteristics merely by wanting or desiring them, as many of his critics have wrongly claimed; his theory was much more mechanical than that. He thought that the urge or need within the organism translated itself into a kind of fluid, which flowed into the organ that needed to change—for example, when a giraffe stretched its neck to reach the leaves.

The "inheritance of acquired characteristics," however, does not hold up well to close examination. Giraffes might succeed in stretching their necks—a little. But what about camouflage coloration: stripes, splotches, or spots? Most animals could not cause a change in coloration by trying or even needing to. Also the evidence did not support the idea that acquired characteristics could be inherited, even if an individual did succeed in changing its anatomy.

But, despite getting sidetracked and being forever stigmatized on this point, Lamarck undeniably brought evolution to the forefront in biological thought, and he was the first biologist of any stature to do so. Erasmus Darwin (the grandfather of Charles Darwin) had put forth the idea some 50 years earlier, but his work was speculative and not really well thought through (a point that always embarrassed his grandson). Cuvier refuted him flatly, preferring the idea of catastrophism (see chapter 3 on geology). Over this point Lamarck quarreled bitterly with Cuvier—and Cuvier, a bad man to cross, never forgave that quarrel.

In his later years Lamarck became blind, and, in a supremely low moment, Cuvier sarcastically chided him, "Perhaps your own refusal to use your eyes to look at nature properly has caused them to stop working." But Lamarck continued to attend scientific meetings on the arm of a daughter, trying to argue his point. "It is not enough to discover and prove a useful truth," he wrote, "it is also necessary to be able to get it recognized." In 1829 he died penniless, with his useful truth still unrecognized. Overall, the excitement Lamarck kindled in his contemporaries as well as those who followed was caused, unfortunately, more by derision than by scientific interest.

Cuvier Tries to Close the Door

Much of that disfavor and derision was thanks to the efforts of his arch-rival, Georges Cuvier, a giant of science in his time, whose formidable powers of observation and deduction won him well-earned acclaim, and whose political shrewdness gained him consistent success and position throughout the divergent regimes through which French politics passed in his lifetime. Because of the power of his stature, Cuvier's ideas totally eclipsed Lamarck's during his generation, as they did Hutton's in the field of geology (see chapter 3).

Cuvier built his opposition to Lamarck's evolutionary ideas upon the solid foundation of his knowledge of comparative anatomy, which led him to think that the functions of all portions of an animal's anatomy and physiology were so completely integrated that no change could take place from generation to generation without disturbing the balance. Any part of an animal's body, Cuvier contended, was intrinsically related to all other parts of its body—with form following function. The shape and utility of one organ suggested to him a constellation of related organs and functions. He could also reconstruct an entire animal lifestyle, literally in his sleep—or at least a famous story maintains that premise.

It seems that late one night (perhaps after a few glasses too many at the local café), one of his students determined to play a prank on Cuvier, appearing at his bedside dressed as a devil. "Cuvier, Cuvier, I have come to eat you," he growled menacingly. To which Cuvier, still half asleep, calmly replied, "All creatures with horns and hooves are herbivores. You can't eat me." Then Cuvier went back to sleep.

The son of a soldier retired from the French army, Georges-Léopold-Frédéric-Dagobert, Baron Cuvier, was born in 1769 in Montbéliard, a little town in Switzerland, to a relatively poor family of French Huguenots who had fled there for safety during the intolerant reign of Louis XIV. (Cuvier's Protestantism never stood in his way, though, in 18th-century France, and the French revolutionaries annexed the area in which he was born in 1793, making Cuvier officially a French citizen.)

Georges Cuvier, masterful comparative anatomist and paleontologist *(Courtesy, Burndy Library)*

A child prodigy encouraged by his mother, Cuvier learned to read at four and entered the Academy of Stuttgart at 14, where his disciplined approach to his studies and his prodigious memory gained him recognition. (It was said that, later in life, he could recite from memory any paragraph from any book in his 19,000-book library.) As a boy Cuvier became particularly fascinated with Buffon's books, which he found on the bookshelves of his uncle, who— like a great many Europeans—was collecting them, volume by volume, as they came out.

After his graduation at the age of 19, Cuvier became a tutor in Normandy to the 13-year-old son of a count. Not only did Cuvier become seriously interested in science at this point in his life, but he also gained many helpful social skills through his contact with a different segment of society, including counts, former generals, and at least one friend of Voltaire. He also met a zoologist, Etienne Geoffroy St.-Hilaire, who in 1795 helped him secure the position of professor of vertebrate zoology at the Museum of Natural History in

Paris. Napoléon, whose successes as a general in the revolutionary wars had won him acclaim, invited Cuvier to accompany him to Egypt in 1798. Cuvier, however, declined. Napoléon liked Cuvier, and when he came to power, first as consul and then as emperor, he found positions for Cuvier in his government. In 1803 Cuvier became permanent secretary of physical and natural sciences of the Institut National, and in 1808 Napoléon put him in charge of investigating education in France. When the Bourbon royal family returned in 1815, Cuvier might as well have lost out; but they used Cuvier instead, making him chancellor of the former Imperial University, now again the University of Paris. Cuvier also served in the cabinet of Louis XVIII, although, when Louis's more reactionary brother, Charles X, succeeded him in 1824, Cuvier had a brief fall from prominence. But by 1831, with Charles X exiled once more, the new king, Louis-Philippe, made him a baron. He also appointed him minister of the interior, although Cuvier did not live long enough to fill that position. He died during a cholera epidemic in May 1832.

Despite his ardent opposition to any hint of evolutionary theory, Cuvier contributed several ideas that made its formulation possible in the 19th century. He was first to think of applying his principles of comparative anatomy to fossils. He recognized that fossils, entombed as they are in rock strata, represent a moment of time in the Earth's history, immobilized for examination. He urged his fellow scientists to ask questions, to examine, to engage in empirical study.

"Naturalists," he harangued, "seem to have scarcely any idea of propriety of investigating facts before they construct their systems."

Collectors had amassed great accumulations of fossils, picked up haphazardly and mindlessly assembled. Cuvier scolded them for regarding their fossil collections "as mere curiosities, rather than historical documents," for neglecting to look at what laws might govern the positions in which they were found or their relation with the strata in which they were found. He set forth a series of questions that he thought needed to be asked, such as "Are there certain animals and plants peculiar to certain strata and not found in others? What are the species that appear first in order, and those that succeed? Do these two kinds of species ever accompany one another?" And so on, in methodical order.

While we might be impressed by the rigor of Cuvier's approach, it is easy to be unimpressed by the fact that he thought he could find clues to the Earth's history in this way, since we take that idea so much for granted today. But, in order to establish a geological record from fossils, the ancient creatures of a particular species had to be found only in the rocks laid down in specific ages. For that to be true, the fossils had to represent extinct species, and that was a very hot issue to Cuvier's time. Many of his contemporaries (including Thomas Jefferson) thought that extinction could not possibly have occurred. Those fossils that represented species currently unknown, they maintained, must represent a species still living somewhere on Earth and as yet undiscovered.

Cuvier developed the ability to reconstruct a whole animal from a few parts. In 1796 he examined the ancient fossil of an elephant-like creature and found that it was neither of the two living species. He showed that the fossil of a South American animal, the *Megatherium,* was a giant ground sloth, now extinct, but related to smaller sloths in existence today. In 1812 he named a great flying reptile a *pterodactyl* because its membrane-wing stretched out along one enormous finger. (In Greek, *pteron* means, "wing," and *daktylos* means "finger.") His explanation of these discoveries was that life's history must reflect a sequence of creations (and extinctions), each one more modern than the last.

Cuvier also refined Linnaeus's system of classification, dividing the animal kingdom into four basic "types" and emphasizing the basically parallel nature of Linnaeus's arrangement. (The parallel ranking had serious consequences for the long-prevalent Great Chain of Being, not to mention Lamarck's hierarchical approach, both of which Cuvier rejected.) The four types represented groupings of animals with similar internal structures, four master plans with infinitely variable external structures adapted to the demands of the environment. Similarities of internal structures, not an ordered ranking of external characteristics, formed the basis for his classifications, and relationships between the species were based on these similarities. (Cuvier was also the first to include fossils in his system of classification.)

Cuvier's work with fossils and his system of classification set the stage, in a way, for Darwin's idea that in natural development a single original form can change in several different ways at once, leading to several kinds of diversification, with the ones best adapted to a specific environment being naturally perpetuated, or selected.

But, despite all this, Cuvier was against evolution. He knew that fossils must be ancient—buried as they were in rocky strata that could only have formed over a great passing of time. And he knew that the deeper the fossil and the older the rock, the greater the differences between the fossils and the modern anatomical structures. He had set up a system of classification that implied diversification from an original model. Why then did he not make the easy leap to evolutionary theory?

Some critics say that Cuvier had a major blind spot: He believed in the biblical account of the Earth's history as recounted in Genesis. But Cuvier maintained that his objections were primarily scientific; based on his knowledge of the way the internal workings of animals fit together, he was sure that the species were fixed and distinct and that evolution was impossible. He also saw in catastrophism an idea he believed explained the existence of ancient fossils and apparently extinct species. Radical Enlightenment materialists, such as La Mettrie and Erasmus Darwin, had speculated about the origin and mutability of life. But the newly discovered facts of comparative anatomy made those concepts seem naive. The reality of biological complexity seemed to preclude the creation of these forms by a natural process.

By the time of Cuvier's death, the 19th-century geologist Charles Lyell had already made a few inroads on his position, though. He strengthened the case for the uniformitarian doctrine—the idea set forth by James Hutton that processes currently occurring on Earth provide a basis for understanding processes that have taken place in the past, the "steady-state" Earth—explaining all the Earth's features on this basis, without needing to resort to catastrophic theory. It was the beginning hint of a revolution to come in the history of biological thought.

Both Lamarck and Cuvier, ironically, are best known for being wrong. Lamarck for his association with the idea of inheritance of acquired characteristics (which he did not originate and which was not central to his thinking). Also Cuvier for his insistence on catastrophism and his belief in the fixity of the species. Both deserve better at the hands of the history of science.

Georges Cuvier was an exacting methodologist, and the brilliance, order, and system he brought to his science produced an effect that far outshone his "mistakes." His dedication and showmanship brought respect and admiration to the search for the understanding that science represents. Charles Lyell, the very man

Cuvier's knowledge of anatomy and bone structure of animals both living and extinct was unparalleled in his time. *(Bettmann/Corbis)*

whose later publications in part produced the downfall of Cuvier's reputation, wrote his description of a visit he paid to Cuvier and his own recognition that the setting Cuvier had created to work in reflected his great involvement in his work, the kind of system and order that it required and the contribution it made to his prodigious output:

> I got into Cuvier's sanctum sanctorum yesterday, and it is truly characteristic of the man. In every part it displays that extraordinary power of methodizing which is the grand secret of the prodigious feats which he performs annually without appearing to give himself the least trouble. . . . There is first the museum of natural history opposite his house, and admirably arranged by himself, then the anatomy museum connected with his dwelling. In the latter is a library disposed in a suite of rooms, each containing works on one subject. There is one where there are all the works on ornithology, in another room all on ichthyology, in another osteology, in another law books! etc., etc. . . . The ordinary studio contains no bookshelves. It is a longish room, comfortably furnished, lighted from above, with eleven desks to stand to, and two low tables . . .

Cuvier's empiricism—his insistence on looking at the results of observation and experiment—embodied everything that was exhilarating about the Age of Reason. Lamarck also ably pointed forward to one of the greatest and most powerful theories of modern science. If about some things they were wrong, they only suffered the burden inevitable to anyone who risks asking questions and daring answers. As science writer Stephen Jay Gould wrote on this subject, "Some types of truth may require pursuit on the straight and narrow, but the pathways to scientific insight are as winding and complex as the human mind." In that statement lie both the challenge and the wonder of science—that truths unfold in a strange and weaving manner—as the scientific adventures yet to come in the 19th century would further demonstrate.

PART III
Science and Society in the 18th Century

10
A Time of Reason and Revolution

SOMETIMES KNOWN AS THE AGE of Confidence, the 18th century was a time of enormous optimism about the power of human reason to discover all ultimate truths and overcome all problems, intellectual, philosophical, and social. All this optimism stemmed in large part from the successes of the preceding century. From the great thinkers of the Scientific Revolution—Nicolaus Copernicus, Galileo Galilei, and Isaac Newton—scientists had inherited a key that seemed capable of unlocking all the secrets of nature. At the dawn of the 18th century, the world—in fact, the entire universe—began to seem altogether knowable.

Of course the farmer tilling his fields, the midwife calmly performing her duties, and the shopkeeper selling his wares had little time left in their crowded days to contemplate the nature of the universe or humankind's place in it. But even the farmer, the midwife, and the merchant, along with millions of others, found that the spirit of the times was changing. Not everyone liked the transformation, and not everyone understood it or accepted it, but by the end of the century it had touched the lives of virtually everyone in the Western world. The 18th century's three great political and socioeconomic revolutions—the American, the French, and the Industrial—were all touched off by this new outlook, and its impact helped to define the world we live in today.

At the heart of this change stood Newton, his *Principia mathematica,* and the natural laws of gravity and motion he uncovered.

Nature, Newton had demonstrated, played by rules—rules that appeared to be regular and identifiable. Nature was no longer seen as a capricious and unpredictable force; instead it was governed by basic laws that it always obeyed. For the thinkers of the 18th century, Newton's discovery of the existence of these laws disclosed a clockwork universe. As shown in earlier chapters of this book, they saw the world—and everything in it—as part of a great machine. Further, they thought one could gain understanding about how the world-machine worked by examining its parts and their relationships and applying common sense and reason, much in the same way that a skilled craftsperson might find out how a clock worked by taking it apart.

Newton, building on the work of Copernicus, Tycho Brahe, Kepler, and Galileo before him, gave the final proof to the power of the scientific method. This new approach to nature had caused an avalanche of consequences in his time. Not only did 17th-century scientists set straight many ancient distortions about the way the physical world worked, but some—most notably the English physiologist William Harvey—also used the new method to discover the internal mechanisms of the human body. Progress in biology occasionally stumbled when scientists applied too strict a "Newtonian" and "mechanistic" interpretation to human physiology, but 18th-century thinkers saw that it was possible to use the scientific method of observation and experimentation to answer many difficult questions successfully. No longer did answers have to come from the books and writings of ancient thinkers or the unchallengeable world of religious authorities.

Reason and Society

This new outlook liberated the thinkers of the 18th century from the authority of ancient Greek theories that had never been tested by experiment or observation. Knowledge of the world, they realized, could be acquired, not passively from Greek and Latin manuscripts and wizened scholars, but from the active, curious, and disciplined engagement of their minds applying rational thinking, observation, and experimentation to a variety of problems.

Was there room in this new "enlightened" view for religion? Newton himself was troubled by this question. Devoutly religious, Newton never gave up his belief in God. He believed, in fact, that it was occasionally necessary for God to intervene to keep the solar system working in its beautiful machinelike precision. Finally he concluded that the wonderful machinery of the universe, in all its clockwork precision, demonstrated the magnificent power and majesty of its creator. In the 18th century, after it was discovered by mathematical analysis that God's intervention was not necessary to keep the solar system stable, many replaced religious beliefs based on revelation and church authority with Deism, a belief in a natural religion based on reason. Deists, who counted Benjamin Franklin and Thomas Jefferson among their numbers, held that God had created the world and all of its natural laws but, having finished the job, had left the machinery to run by itself. As Newton had foreseen, though, this view left some people wondering whether a clockwork universe required the existence of God at all. Consequently—and this possibility had troubled Newton—some of the Enlightenment thinkers became atheists, denying the need for or existence of any god. One group especially, the philosophes in France, strove to build a moral philosophy based not on revealed religion but on human ethical thought. Their ranks included such great thinkers as Voltaire, Diderot, and Montesquieu. So, while by far the vast majority remained theists, maintaining their allegiance to God and the traditional teachings of religion about miracles, Newton's legacy also introduced new doubts about fundamental issues of religion and philosophy.

The celebration of reason presented new questions about social structure and values as well. Scientists had discovered that nature had "natural laws." Was it possible that similar natural "laws" might govern all moral, social, and political activities? If that was the case, many believed, then by applying rational thinking, those laws could also be discovered and turned toward the benefit of humanity. Philosophers such as Immanuel Kant (who coined the term *enlightenment* to describe the new dawn of reason and the intellectual brilliance of the time), David Hume, Gottfried Wilhelm Leibniz, François Marie Arouet (known as Voltaire), Jean-Jacques Rousseau, and others sought to find a place for humanity in the new scientific-sociopolitical views. Writers brought the new ideas of science and philosophy to the general public through an enormous output of publications. One of the most influential publications was the massive 35-volume *Encyclopédie ou dictionnaire raisonné des sciences, des arts et des métiers* (Encyclopedia or systematic dictionary of sciences, arts, and trades), started by French journalist-philosopher Denis Diderot.

Thomas Jefferson exemplified many of the currents of thought in the 18th century—from the politics of individual rights, to the philosophy of freedom and concern for balance in government, to personal involvement in the scientific process and a belief in the human capacity for progress. *(Courtesy of the National Library of Medicine)*

In Paris, writers, philosophers, and artists gathered at *salons* in the homes of wealthy and intelligent French women who invited them to meet there and exchange views. It was a time when lively, impassioned, and closely reasoned discussions flew among the philosophers, not only at the salons of Paris, but also in lengthy correspondence in which a number of women also took part. Few women were permitted the education needed to contribute in more direct ways, but a notable exception in these circles was Emilie du Châtelet, whose translation of the work of Newton from Latin to French was responsible for its wide dissemination and much of its influence in France. Several women, including Laura Bassi, Caroline Herschel, and Marie-Anne Lavoisier, took an active part in the advances of science in the 1700s.

The new thinking of the Enlightenment burst like fireworks across the social, geographical, and political boundaries of the Western world. Across the Atlantic, in the American colonies, it kindled the thinking of political leaders and molders of government such as Thomas Jefferson, Thomas Paine, and scientist-statesman-author Benjamin Franklin. Jefferson, as well as many other intelligent and well-read people of the 18th century, particularly felt the influence of the English philosopher John Locke (1632–1704). In his work *An Essay Concerning Human Understanding,* published in 1689, Locke declared that there were natural laws constructed by God to ensure the happiness and welfare of humanity. Paramount among those laws were the rights of life, liberty, and property. Furthermore, Locke argued, while people originally lived in a state of nature free from restriction or restraint, the strong had violated that peaceful existence and taken unfair advantage over the weak. To defend themselves from such cruelty and enjoy their God-given rights, people had chosen rulers under special agreements. In exchange for the ruler's protection and aid in holding on to their natural rights, they had agreed to abide by the ruler's decision and dictates. If a ruler began to violate those natural rights, though, Locke argued, then the people had the right to disobey and, if necessary, to overthrow that ruler.

In England the idea of natural human rights had already grown strong during the 17th century, as Parliament struggled to wrest power away from an autocratic monarchy. In 1628 Parliament forced Charles I to sign the Petition of Right, which required approval of taxes by Parliament, established limitations on military law, and held that no person could be imprisoned without a specific charge. In a civil war beginning in 1642, following several despotic moves by Charles, Parliament overthrew the king, replacing the monarchy with a republic headed by Puritan general Oliver Cromwell. But the revolution faltered at Cromwell's death in 1658, and in 1660 Parliament invited Charles II, son of the executed king, to take the throne. But Parliament took control again in 1688. In a move known as the Glorious Revolution, Parliament offered the crown to the king's Protestant daughter Mary and her husband, William of Orange, over her Catholic brother James, who was next in line. In 1689, the year Locke published his *Essay*, Parliament drew up what is known as the English Bill of Rights. The effect was the establishment of parliamentary government, rule by law, limited monarchy, and the protection of individual liberties. These events in England, combined with the influence of the Scientific Revolution, had great effect on government in the Western world.

Many French thinkers in the 18th century admired the English government and strove to develop philosophies of human government, education, and society that reflected reasoned and just policies, based on an understanding of the essence of what it means to be human. These philosophies also left a powerful mark on the intellectual climate of the time. They promoted reform in France, reacting against the excesses of the absolute monarchy that ruled there. They objected to preferences given to nobility, who paid few taxes and received the best positions by right of birth. The philosophes rankled against the special rights accorded the Catholic Church in

France, which paid no taxes and had the right to censor books, restricting their publication (as it had done the century before in Italy when it placed Galileo's *Dialogue on the Two Chief Systems of the World* on the Index of Forbidden Books).

Some, such as the baron de Montesquieu, despite his privileged social position as an aristocrat, focused on formulating governmental policies that would ensure individual rights for all. Montesquieu suggested the principle of separation of powers, dividing authority among three branches of government, a system that greatly influenced the authors of the Constitution of the United States. He maintained that, by separating the legislative, executive, and judicial powers, no one entity would ever have absolute authority.

The philosophes supported Locke's view that people were born neither good nor evil, and that a child's mind was like a blank tablet on which no one has written. Nine out of 10 people, wrote Locke, "are good or evil, useful or not, [as a result of] their education." The idea had profound political implications—that people should have no special treatment by right of birth, only on the basis of their ability to contribute, which depended on their education. Society could produce good citizens through good education.

Across the ocean Jefferson and his colleagues would borrow many of Locke's ideas when the American colonies sought to free themselves from the economic and political encumbrance of British rule. The American Declaration of Independence, which echoed many of Locke's ideas, the American Revolution of 1776, the American Bill of Rights, and the democratic government that replaced the colonial regime all reflect Locke's influence.

In Europe, many 18th-century monarchs such as Prussia's Frederick II (1712–86) saw themselves as "enlightened rulers." Often, though, these rulers only paid lip service to the new ideas on human rights sweeping around them. Meanwhile they continued to hold a tight grip on the lives of the people they saw as their subjects, showing attitudes held over from the medieval days of serfdom, when kings felt they owned their subjects and all they produced.

In France, the home of some of the greatest Enlightenment thinkers and scientists, change came later, and when it came it was violent, confused, and bloody. Change was long overdue, and the French were not content to watch English and American citizens enjoy the implementation of human rights while their own society still labored under an outdated feudal system, plagued with eco-

Typical of the aristocracy of the age, Frederick II of Prussia embraced the ideals of the Enlightenment without recognizing that, fully extended, those ideals would mean the end of monarchs and nobility. Considering himself a great friend of science, here Frederick welcomes philosophe and encyclopedist Jean d'Alembert to Berlin. (*Figuier,* Vies des savants, *1870*)

nomic inequality, special class privileges, and the absolute rule of kings. At the same time that the philosophes were writing about equal rights, the French bourgeoisie, or middle class, was growing stronger, more well-to-do, and more ambitious; the peasants and city workers lived in poverty; and the nobles sought even more power. France, meanwhile, faced a grave economic crisis. King Louis XIV, who died in 1715, had spent lavishly on luxurious living and wars. In his wake he left enormous debts. Those who followed, Louis XV and Louis XVI, borrowed more and spent even more lavishly. Because the church and the nobility were largely protected from taxation, and even most of the wealthy bourgeoisie were exempt, the only sources of revenue were the poverty-stricken peasants and city workers. In June 1789 the bourgeoisie tried to change the order of government by establishing a new legislative body called the National Assembly. But revolt was inevitable. On July 14, 1789, Parisians massed outside the Bastille, the great fortress prison that symbolized the monarchy's injustices and oppression. The angry mob stormed the prison, killing the commander and some of the guards; the Revolution had begun and the bloodshed did not stop for years. Louis XVI was sent to the guillotine in January 1793. His wife, Marie Antoinette, was executed

John Kay and the Flying Shuttle

One of the most influential of the earliest inventions of the Industrial Revolution was John Kay's flying shuttle. Patented in 1733 the machine was an improvement on the weaver's loom. Before Kay's invention two weavers were needed to weave a wide piece of cloth. Each would stand on opposite sides of the loom and toss the shuttle back and forth across the width of the cloth. Kay's invention was simple. He mounted his shuttle on small rollers so that it would roll back and forth on a wooden rail. One weaver then could quickly move it from side to side by pulling on a chord that caused wooden hammers to hit it back and forth.

While the invention increased the speed of the weaving and made it possible to weave wider cloth than had been woven before, it also eliminated one of the two weavers previously needed for the job. That was not a happy situation for the weavers of Colchester, where Kay first introduced his invention. They argued that Kay was trying to take their jobs away the same year. A period known as the Reign of Terror began, and between September 1793 and July 1794 at least 20,000 people (possibly even twice that many) were executed.

When the bloodshed finally ended, a new constitution was adopted, in 1795. Now France, too, enjoyed a new constitutional government established according to many of the Enlightenment principles of the philosophes—including guarantees of individual rights. When Napoléon Bonaparte came to power in 1799 as first consul, he established a new system of laws, the Code Napoléon, based on the ideals of the Revolution.

The Nascent Power of Technology

Meanwhile another kind of transformation—the mechanization of production known as the Industrial Revolution—began to change the shape of the economic world. The Industrial Revolution began about 1750–60, primarily in Great Britain, where a combination of factors, including advances in agriculture, converged to make dramatic changes possible—changes that had both positive and negative effects. In 1701 a man named Jethro Tull invented a mechanical seeder. A

from them. Kay argued that more weavers would be needed to produce even more cloth than had been produced before, but that did not settle the problem of the weavers, who were afraid that until the demand for cloth increased, they would still be out of work.

Kay took his machines to Leeds, hoping to drum up some interest there, but his luck took another bad turn. The manufacturers at Leeds liked the machine but refused to pay him royalties for its use. His lawsuits against them proved practically useless when they united and fought him in the courts, costing him most of his money in heavy court expenses.

Disheartened and nearly broke Kay returned to his native town of Bury, England, in 1745. The flying shuttle had caught on and begun to replace weavers across England. Even though he was not making money with his invention, groups of angry laborers rioted and broke into his house, looting it and forcing him to flee. He escaped to Manchester, but eventually he was also forced to flee that city, hiding in a sack of wool. Feeling unsafe in England, Kay emigrated to France, where he died penniless.

horse-drawn hoe soon followed, and, as a result, food production increased so dramatically that Great Britain could now feed its growing population without importing as much food as before, thus freeing up financial resources to import raw materials for other kinds of production. In its colonies Britain had good sources of supply, especially for cotton, and good markets for manufactured products.

The textile industry, which relied at the time on hundreds of weavers and spinners isolated in their cottages, was the first to be dramatically transformed by a series of inventions. In 1733 John Kay invented the flying shuttle to speed weaving—with the result that one weaver could use all the thread produced by several spinners. In the 1760s James Hargreaves invented what he called a spinning jenny, a device that enabled a spinner to turn a series of spindles by using a single spinning wheel. The power that ran both these "machines" was still human power, but by 1769 Richard Arkwright had figured out how to use waterpower to run a spinning machine, and by 1785 Edmund Cartwright had invented a loom run by waterpower. Now the weak point in production was obtaining enough raw materials to supply the speeding spinners and weavers, especially cotton fiber, which holds its seeds tangled tightly among its strands. But in 1793 an American inventor, Eli Whitney, solved that problem with the invention of his cotton gin, which stripped the seeds out automatically.

By now the new machines began to be too expensive for individual weavers to rent or own, and with the new use of waterpower, it became necessary to have a source of running water nearby for weaving and spinning. So entrepreneurs began to build and organize factories for efficient production, purchasing the equipment, hiring workers, and locating new markets for the goods. Textile manufacturers began to replace the cottage industry they had always relied on with a vastly more efficient factory system. The result was more goods produced more quickly—and they were cheaper and more readily available, an advance from which everyone profited.

Advances in iron production and Eli Whitney's concept of standard interchangeable parts for manufacturing machinery made the development of machinery more efficient, too. As already mentioned, by 1769 James Watt had developed the first practical steam engine. Now, because England had excellent coal and iron-ore resources, a cheap source of power was available to streamline almost every industry.

The social effects, however, were not all positive. Factory owners expected long hours of intensive, repetitive work. Working conditions were unpleasant and unsafe, and children, who had always worked alongside their parents in the cottage industries, were employed by the factories and exposed to many hazardous conditions. Workers no longer enjoyed the freedom and independence of working at home, and they spent large portions of every day in unpleasant surroundings under the watchful eye of a factory boss. Reforms were long in coming, and much of the bucolic life of the British countryside was transformed into a series of sprawling, increasingly noisy and dirty industrial towns and cities. But reforms did come eventually, people learned how to use the new technologies more humanely, and the Industrial Revolution produced enormous improvements to the general standard of living. In addition the technologies that put these changes in motion set the stage for many more advances—including electricity—that would arrive in the following century.

11
Champions of Science
Popularizing Reason

THE SPIRIT OF THE 18TH CENTURY was so rich with ideas and new achievements that a great publishing project was born in France about mid-century. This publication would grow to become a vast and powerful compendium of knowledge, but it gained its start from a much more modest plan. In the beginning an English entrepreneur named John Mills approached the king's printer, André Le Breton, in Paris. The idea Mills proposed was to publish a French translation of an existing English encyclopedia, Ephraim Chambers's *Cyclopaedia*. The *Cyclopedia* was clearly presented and well written, and Le Breton agreed to the plan. Later, though, Mills and Le Breton had a falling out, and Mills withdrew from the undertaking. Le Breton found another editor and hired a couple of underlings to check the translations. Even though it was not obvious at the time, one of those underlings would turn out to be a key player in the growth of the movement in France known as the Enlightenment. His name was Denis Diderot.

Diderot and the Encyclopedists

Born in Langres, France, on October 5, 1713, Diderot studied a variety of subjects in Paris from 1729 to 1732. He soaked up everything—theater, mathematics, languages, law, literature, philosophy. He had an active mind and a face that lit up when discussions turned to philosophy and the promise for a bright future that he saw in rational thought. Like many of his contemporaries, he thought that right reason, or rational thinking, would naturally lead to expanded human knowledge, progress, and happiness.

In 1745, when Le Breton offered Diderot a modest contract as translator, the younger man was 32 years old, a bourgeois freelance author who was struggling to support his family—and keep a mistress happy who constantly worried him for money. At the outset he was grateful just to have a steady income. However, before long he began to envision a much more ambitious project—a completely new, French *Encyclopédie*. The idea of an encyclopedia was not in itself a new idea—throughout the Middle

Denis Diderot, who began his career as a nondescript freelance writer, became the founding editor of the *Encyclopédie,* which he envisioned, structured, and guided to become the bulkhead of the Enlightenment, a manifesto (in many volumes) of progress, and a hymn to the value of knowledge of every kind. *(Stock Montage Inc.)*

Ages many compilers of knowledge had laboriously gathered information and copied it into volume after volume. But this one would be different. Experts in each field would write current, up-to-date descriptions and discussions of the latest in science, philosophy, culture, literature, mathematics, history, and—for the first time—the trades. Respected mathematician Jean Le Rond d'Alembert joined the editorial staff as second in command. Le Breton was soon sold on the new venture, which he saw as a sound investment with strong potential for profit.

Officially known as *Encyclopédie, ou dictionnaire raissoné de sciences, des arts et des métiers* (Encyclopedia, or systematic dictionary of sciences, arts, and trades), the *Encyclopédie* quickly broadened in scope. The emphasis on the trades was unique, a facet of the work that Diderot felt contributed an element of basic, sound usefulness. Diderot put together a team of "encyclopedists" who offered depth of expertise, dedication, eloquence, and philosophical complexity. They included such powerful literary figures as Voltaire, Jean-Jacques

Rousseau, and Montesquieu; key scientists such as Buffon; and even a few priests. Opinions expressed were outspoken and daring, setting forth the advanced, radical, even revolutionary ideas of the time in the fields of religion, politics, and philosophy. These philosophes flew the banner of knowledge, and their rallying cry called for abandonment of reactionary ideas. Their cause relied on the power of the pen against the forces in church and state that would sound a retreat. The *Encyclopédie* was to be a *dictionnaire raisonné* (rational dictionary) that would explore the applications of every art and science, but it also had a polemical purpose: to put forth the philosophical tenets of the Enlightenment, celebrating the philosophy of rationalism and the progress of the human mind, and to defeat the enemies of a cause they felt was at the very heart of what it meant to be human.

With Diderot as editor, the *Encyclopédie* came out in 28 volumes between 1751 and 1772 (another seven volumes came out later), including many volumes devoted entirely to plates—engravings illustrating aspects of the trades, botany, physiology, tools, and technology—an aspect of the work upon which Diderot had insisted. However, publication of the first volume did not meet with universal praise. The encyclopedists had stirred up many issues, and both church and state, as well as many readers in general, reacted with anger. How could these philosophers presume to say that nature has no mystery that cannot be made plain through reason? The church knew the power of the pen and knew it to be a threat. The iconoclastic tone of the writing put those in government on notice as well.

So when the first volumes appeared in 1751, both the French government and church censors immediately banned it for encouraging a spirit of revolt, as well as promoting "moral corruption, . . . irreligion, and . . . unbelief."

Jean le Rond d'Alembert, Diderot's second in command, responsible for envisioning the organization of the *Encyclopédie* and author of many articles. *(Courtesy of the National Library of Medicine)*

Diderot insisted on copious illustrations for the *Encyclopédie,* including illustrations such as this plate of tools from a lensmaker's shop. Generally considered too lowly for literary attention, the technologies used in the trades received rare attention under Diderot's direction. *(Courtesy of the National Library of Medicine)*

The Struggle to Be Heard

To some degree every newspaper newsroom in the world confronts the same dilemma faced by Diderot and the encyclopedists: to censor oneself so that the power to censor does not go to someone else—or to tell the truth plainly, to express an unpopular opinion, without self-censorship, and face the consequences. Whatever one's opinion of their politics and philosophy, one can see that the encyclopedists were courageous and passionate about their cause. They paid for those courageous acts. Diderot wrote several books and essays on the side while serving as editor for the *Encyclopédie*. He knew they were inflammatory, and he did not put his name on some of them. Yet no one was fooled. The police came to his door one morning as he was sitting down to begin his work, and they took him away to jail (to the great distress of Le Breton, who envisioned his entire investment lost without the captain of the encyclopedists at the helm). Diderot was lucky. He did get out. Early in his career Voltaire, meanwhile, spent a year imprisoned in the Bastille for writing a few satirical poems that offended people in power, and later he went into exile in England for three years. Because the government controlled all printing in France, censorship came easily. Works by Montesquieu, atheist Paul Henri d'Holbach, Claude Helvétius, and others were all suppressed.

Censorship also came sometimes from within. Buffon and others sometimes wrote flagrantly and then later retracted what they said. An interesting volume of the *Encyclopédie* turned up for sale recently that reveals a look at the process that took place between pen and printing press. It is the 18th-century equivalent of page proofs edited in Diderot's

Diderot finally convinced the censors to release some of the volumes, but many of the articles had to be carefully worded to avoid arousing their anger again. Publication continued and, in all, some 35 volumes finally appeared.

Voltaire and the Case for Reason

Voltaire was a few years older than the upstart editor of the *Encyclopédie*. He was born in Paris on November 21, 1694, with the name François Marie Arouet, which he later traded for his pen name. Educated by Jesuit teachers and raised by freethinkers, his acerbic wit handwriting—an apparent attempt to undo editing done by Le Breton before going to press in an effort to tone down the writing so it would not attract the ire of church officials, the Jesuits, and the police.

To the extent that stating an unpopular idea no longer carries such severe penalties, perhaps we have attained some of that human progress for which the Encyclopedists and philosophes fought so hard.

A group of encyclopedists gather at Diderot's home. *(Stock Montage Inc.)*

and razor-sharp thought processes reflected his background. He is considered by many to have been the most influential of the philosophes of the Enlightenment.

Voltaire's literary output was prodigious in every genre, but today he is best known for his essays, short stories, and novels, in which he put across many of his ideas. Voltaire was the enemy of unreason wherever he found it—in the church, in government, in all examples of intolerance. He railed against injustices in the tax system, in the prisons and judicial system, and in censorship. He referred to the opposition as *l'infâme* (the infamous), in his famous slogan *Ecrasez l'infâme!* (Crush the infamous).

To anyone keeping score the early half of the century was tough on the philosophes and their causes. The battle was mostly uphill. Yet their impact did pay off. The government established in the United States reflected the thoughts of Montesquieu and Jefferson and Franklin—all of them Enlightenment figures. The philosophes began to gain admission to honorary societies and academies. A vast upswing in newspaper and book publication made for a better informed public and wider acceptance of new ideas. However, for every increase in enlightened thinking, darker crosscurrents and undercurrents seemed to run—then as now—all the deeper.

12

Dark Countercurrents
Charlatans and Quacks

NOT ALL OF WESTERN CIVILIZATION was enlightened by the Enlightenment. As historian Norman Hampton wrote, ". . . if the Enlightenment was a product of the 18th century, the 18th century was not a product of the Enlightenment." Superstition and mysticism still held sway over much of 18th century life. Folktales, folk medicine, myths, and magic still dominated the thinking of farmers and the rural poor. Charlatans, confidence tricksters, and quack physicians plied their trades in the bustling city streets. In the mansions, palaces, and elegant apartments of the aristocrats and socially elite, increasing wealth and boredom lead to a quest for the novel and bizarre.

The new view of the world brought forth by Newton made people uneasy. The idea of a mechanized universe, governed by the inflexible laws of physics, was repellent to them. Many clung tenaciously to the church, if with somewhat less conviction than before. And many turned to the supposed comfort of the past—seeking out the psychological safety net of stern and rigid but reliable rules and rituals. More than a few 18th-century intellectuals sought solace in what they saw as the romantic life of the Middle Ages, with its colorful tales of honorable knights and heroic quests.

Membership swelled among secret societies such as the Freemasons and Rosicrucians, as they in turn became more mystical and mysterious in their initiations and rituals. Dozens of breakaway societies and sects romanticizing Arthurian knights, ancient alchemical secrets, and "forgotten wisdom" sprang up in big cities and small hamlets alike.

The age of Voltaire, Diderot, and Franklin was also the age of Alessandro, conte di Cagliostro; Emanuel Swedenborg; and Franz Mesmer. Scientific and rational thinkers shared the stage with psychics and seers. While Swedenborg and Mesmer started their careers as scientists and ended up as mystics, Cagliostro and other confidence tricksters, such as the so-called Saint-Germain, never made pretensions toward scientific thinking. Being neither advocates for reason nor honest believers in religious thought, Cagliostro and his fellows mystified the minds of their followers and filled their own pocketbooks with the profits of the public's gullibility.

Cagliostro, whose real name is believed to have been Giovanni Balsanno, was probably born in Palermo, Italy, in 1743. Historians have called him the "arch quack" of his age. Moving among the capital cities of Europe, there was scarcely a mystical talent that Cagliostro didn't claim. He could, he said, call the ancient Egyptian dead from their graves, transmute metal into gold, foresee the future, heal the sick, discover secret treasures, and, like his contemporary the mysterious Saint-Germain, perhaps live forever—or at least for three or four centuries. Needless to say this last talent he was willing to share with his many wealthy and influential admirers. Of course, there was a price attached. The price meant little, though, to those who could afford it, and the wonderful elixir, personally concocted by Cagliostro, also bought that elegant and extravagant charlatan access to the best drawing rooms of the wealthy and well-connected. No street-corner huckster, Cagliostro plied his devious trade even in the palaces of royalty. His downfall came, ironically, with a probably innocent involvement in a notorious confidence game involving a necklace belonging to the queen of France—which eventually lead to his imprisonment.

Even less is known of Cagliostro's contemporary known only as the Comte Saint-Germain. Like Cagliostro, Saint-Germain made his home, or homes, among Europe's wealthy and elite. His many followers believed in rumors that he was centuries old, rumors that Saint-Germain did little to discourage. Once, when his valet was asked if it was true that Saint-Germain was 700 years old, the valet replied that he did not know, since he himself had only been with Saint-Germain for 200 years. Like Cagliostro, Saint-Germain also pushed his magic elixirs, professing powers of healing and psychic abilities. Many said that he had actually discovered the "Philosopher's Stone," the prime objective of the alchemists' quest—a stone they believed could not only transmute metal to gold but would also give human beings the powers, wisdom, and longevity of the ancient gods.

Both Cagliostro and the Comte Saint-Germain claimed association with the Freemasons or, more specifically, with elite and secret cadres within that society. Although it is doubtful that such secret cadres actually existed within the Freemasons, simply evoking their existence helped Cagliostro and Saint-Germain establish their credibility among the gullible. For many in the 18th century, the Freemasons represented a link to the supposed mysteries and powers of the ancient and mystical past.

The origin and activities of the Freemasons are clouded by myth and legends, some originating with the Freemasons themselves and some conceived in the romantic and sensational notions of writers and journalists. However, claims that the society of Freemasons can be traced back to ancient Egypt, or even earlier, fall short. The first known written mention of the Freemasons appears in official records of the city of London in 1375.

Historians have concluded that the Society of Freemasons began during the 14th century as a guild of skilled stonecutters and builders who sought to protect their local interests by organizing themselves into the guild and its local "lodges." The skills of stonemasons were a premium commodity when it came to building towering monuments and great cathedrals, so they often enjoyed positions and freedoms usually withheld from other, more lowly workers. Often during the Middle Ages, they participated in the architectural design of the projects and buildings they worked on. Of necessity they protected the secrets of their trade. Outsiders, interlopers, and pretenders could bring ruin to the craft and to the skilled craftsmen by offering shoddy work at lower prices. To protect themselves from such intrusions, the masons adopted secret signs and signals by which they could recognize one another when working among strangers in strange lands or hiring extra skilled help for their projects when it was needed.

As the age of great cathedral building ended in the 17th century, the masons began to open up membership in their society to interested outsiders who could pay double the usual fee for membership. Although the first outsiders to join were from the privileged class of wealth or social standing, the Freemasons' democratic ideology that stressed individual qualities over social position soon drew many freethinkers and intellectuals into the fold. With the admittance of such outsiders who did not work within the stonemasonry profession, the masons gradually became less a guild of craftsmen and more a social and fraternal organization. For many outside the Masonic society, though, the Masons still represented an elite group who were privy to long-preserved secrets of the past. Many also believed that these Masonic secrets encompassed much more than stonework, touching upon mystical and magical skills long sought by alchemists and magicians.

Unfortunately, while many of the local lodges became centers of progressive, democratic ideas, more than a few others capitalized on the alleged reputation for alchemy and magic. This segment of the society enticed new members by stressing the mystical and occult in their initiations and activities. By associating themselves in the public mind with this occult aspect of 18th-century Freemasonry, charlatans and confidence artists like Cagliostro and Saint-Germain rode the coattails of Freemasonry and added fuel to its mystical and occult legend.

The search for a satisfying spiritual system—whether religious, mystical, or occult—that would transcend what some saw as the disheartening mechanistic universe of Newton occupied many people in the 18th century. While many philosophers, scientists, and intellectuals were content to adopt a Deist stance with regard to religion, others remained uncomfortable and sought what they hoped would be deeper and more encompassing connections between their lives and the universe.

Emanuel Swedenborg was such a seeker. Born in Stockholm, Sweden, in 1688, he was the child of a Swedish Royal chaplain and became a professional consultant to the mining industry. Highly respected as a scientist, he founded Sweden's first scientific journal

Emanuel Swedenborg, a scientist turned mystic *(Courtesy of the National Library of Medicine)*

and published many papers on cosmology, chemistry, physics, physiology, and psychology. For nearly two-thirds of his life, Swedenborg was a model of the dedicated and productive scientist. No wonder then that many of his peers were shocked when in his 70s Swedenborg announced to the world that Jesus Christ had appeared to him in dreams and instructed him to abandon his scientific pursuits and turn instead to religious revelations.

Swedenborg obeyed his visions and during the remainder of his long life, he turned out more than 30 books revealing the secrets of God and the heavens. What eventually evolved was a complex, sometimes self-contradictory, not always coherent, and often fantastic vision of the universe, Swedenborgian style. While there is no doubt of Swedenborg's essential honesty and sincerity (he was certainly no charlatan of the Cagliostro mold), his reports of further visions and adventures among angels and spirits had many of his acquaintances shaking their heads. He had, he claimed, visited heaven and hell, talked with God face to face, and visited the planets. He described the inhabitants of Venus; some, he said, were kind and benevolent, and others were cruel and gigantic. Moon people, he explained, were no larger than small children but possessed great strength and booming voices. He said he had received the gifts of clairvoyance, mediumship, and special sensory perceptions. Not neglecting his old scientific world, he even laid claim to conversing with the spirit of Newton.

Was Swedenborg mad, a harmless eccentric, or a true visionary? These questions came up often, and his readers, of whom there were many thousands, were left to decide their own answers. What is certain is that many people who had become confused and uncomfortable with the changes brought by the new thinking of the Enlightenment found solace and comfort in Swedenborg's theology and churches based on his "spirituality" and "New Christian religion." His ideas continue to hold the same appeal for many people today.

Like Swedenborg, Anton Mesmer began his career as a scientist. Unlike Swedenborg, he went to his grave still calling himself one— although many disagreed with his self-evaluation.

Franz Anton Mesmer was born in 1734 in the small village of Iznang, near Konstanz, Germany. His father was a gamekeeper for a Catholic bishop and little is known about Mesmer's childhood except that he was one of nine children and his mother apparently had encouraged a few of those children to enter the Catholic

Anton Mesmer claimed that people could be healed through the practice of "animal magnetism." *(Courtesy of the National Library of Medicine)*

Church. History records that one at least, Johann, later became a Catholic priest. Franz Anton, the third to be born, began his schooling in 1743 in a school run by local monks, and in 1750 he left the monastic school to attend the University of Dillingen in Bavaria. There he studied philosophy for four years, showing a particular interest in Descartes. Then he moved on to the University of Ingolstadt, where he studied theology under the Jesuits. After concluding those studies and having no desire to enter the church as a priest, Mesmer moved to the University of Vienna in 1759 intending to study law. A year later, in 1760, he switched again, this time to medicine, and he graduated from medical school in 1767 at the age of 32.

Somewhere along the way Mesmer had developed a fascination for the writings of Paracelsus, and Mesmer's dissertation, written in Latin, was entitled *Disseratio Physico-medica de Planetarum Influxa,* (A physico-medical inquiry concerning the influences of the planets). Later in his life he generally referred to this dissertation as "The Influence of the Planets on the Human Body." Deeply influenced by the cosmological theories of Paracelsus, the thesis sought to scientifically establish a connection between the influence of the heavenly bodies and human health.

Opinions vary about when and where Mesmer first developed the idea that would soon change his life. What is known is that in 1768, he married an extremely wealthy and socially adept woman named Maria Anna von Posch. Older than Mesmer, Maria was well known in Vienna society for hosting lavish parties and fashionable salons where wealthy Viennese women met to discuss fashionable topics of interest. Already something of a favorite in high society, after his marriage Mesmer quickly became a leading figure among Vienna's elite, numbering among his friends the Mozart family and their son, the precocious young musical genius, Wolfgang, or Wolferl, as his family called him.

It was while talking to a wealthy patient who claimed to have been previously treated successfully with magnets that Mesmer first connected the even then questionable use of magnets in the treatment of illness with the theories of cosmology that he had picked up from Paracelsus. Since Paracelsus had also claimed success in attracting diseases from his patients with a magnet and then discharging those diseases into the ground, Mesmer began seeking a theory that might successfully unite his ideas about the planetary influence on human health with the use of magnets in medical treatment.

The somewhat obscure and jumbled "theory" that resulted from his thinking found him postulating that perhaps some kind of universal "magnetic fluid" or force permeated all human bodies, in much the same way as a universal fluid permeated the universe connecting all the heavenly bodies in perfect harmony. Disturbances in this flow resulted in illness, but regulation of the flow within the body could be accomplished by the use of magnetism acting upon this invisible "fluid." It was a crazy idea even then (unfortunately some people still believe it today) and immediately met resistance from Mesmer's peers. Not one to be stopped by criticism, or even to be slowed down by self-criticism—as much as Mesmer liked to think of himself as a scientist—he began treating his patients with magnets.

It wasn't long before Mesmer began to claim some astonishing successes and an even more astounding discovery. Magnets, he announced, were really not responsible for his patients' miraculous cures. He himself was. The magnets, he decided, were not the agents of the cure but merely the conductors of it. The cure came from a "superabundance" of "animal magnetism" that he himself possessed and that transmitted itself through the magnets, balancing out the disturbed "animal magnetism" in his patients.

Needless to say not many of Mesmer's fellow physicians warmed to his new "discovery," although it brought an even larger flock of bored and discontented society women to his doors. A forceful and commanding presence with penetrating eyes and total self-confidence, Mesmer soon found his waiting rooms filled with society's elite waiting to be "cured." All that was required of his patients (other than their money) was their complete and unwavering confidence in his abilities. Once that was given, claimed Mesmer, he could cure anyone. It was an extravagant claim, and one bound to lead to trouble. Trouble, and the end of Mesmer's days in Vienna, came in the form of one Mademoiselle Paridis. Unlike most of his patients, who suffered from minor illnesses, Mademoiselle Paridis was blind.

To make a long, scandal-ridden, and complicated story short, Mesmer failed in his treatments. And to make matters even worse, he failed to accept responsibility for his own failure. If Mademoiselle Paridis failed to see, announced Mesmer, it was because she had failed, not he. She obviously preferred to remain blind. While a few foolish followers supported Mesmer in the scandal, business dropped off and he decided to move on to greener pastures.

The greener pasture in this case was Paris. In 1778 Mesmer moved to the city on the Seine. Home to Voltaire, Descartes, and Dideroit, Paris—as if to show its cosmopolitan magnanimity—also provided a haven for cranks, charlatans, and imposters. The year before Mesmer's arrival, a secret society called the Illuminati had set up its headquarters there, while other so-called secret societies such as the Freemasons continued to flourish in the city's freewheeling intellectual and artistic atmosphere. In the city where Saint-Germain and Cagliostro flourished, there certainly had to be room for Mesmer.

Business was slow at first, but Mesmer soon found support from a wealthy patron, and business began to pick up. It wasn't long before talk of Doctor Mesmer and his wonderful new discovery filled the salons. "Mesmerism" became the fad of the hour, "animal magnetism" the subject of conversation in the finest drawing rooms. The good doctor was in his glory. And he lived his part to the hilt.

Many proponents of the new "scientific thinking" believed that science would drive superstition and the occult into the dustbin of history. Quacks and charlatans, they believed, would disappear under the withering rigor of science. False prophets, alchemists, and seers would vanish, and scientific and rational thinking would prevail. Unfortunately they underestimated the human need for wonder and amazement and the gullibility of those who really wanted to believe in a world not bound by the laws of nature and physics. And they underestimated the cleverness of people who were willing to take advantage of those needs.

Also the world legitimately seemed filled with wonders scientific and technological, and many people had difficulty differentiating between what was science and what was not. For many it really didn't matter. Wonder was wonder and amazement was amazement. What was the difference, people thought, between Benjamin Franklin and others demonstrating the wonders of electricity—with displays of electric kisses and electrified boys—and the wonders of Dr. Mesmer and his amazing "animal magnetism"?

And what a show Dr. Mesmer put on. He had certainly learned much by moving to Paris. Dressed in long flowing robes, looking very much like a charlatan to disbelievers and a true prophet to believers, he walked among his patients with a godly and benevolent hand.

To accommodate his many patients, he outfitted his extravagant apartment with special healing quarters. In the center of those quarters was Mesmer's famous "baquet," or tub, a device Mesmer guaranteed to be truly scientific yet considered magical by many. The tub, four feet in diameter and a foot deep, held wine bottles of "magnetized water," corks facing outward toward the patients. Once the bottles were in place, the tub was filled with plain water and sometimes sprinkled with iron filings before being fitted with a cover containing a number of holes from which iron rods protruded. Sitting around the tub, each patient would hold the end of one of the

Clients gathered around Mesmer's magnetic pool *(Courtesy of the National Library of Medicine)*

rods and wait for the power that would surge through the rod and effect the cure. To help matters along, Mesmer himself would appear, magnificently robed and holding an iron wand. Occasionally he would reach down and touch a patient, adding his own powerful "animal magnetism" to the total effect.

Stories of Mesmer's wondrous tub raced through the best parts of Parisian society. To make matters even more exciting, not only had miraculous cures been effected, but also other more interesting effects were hinted at. Strange things happened around the tub and in Dr. Mesmer's powerful presence. Both men and women seemed to lose all their inhibitions, and sometimes people seemed to be possessed by the strangest behavior.

Mesmer was the rage of Paris. But he wanted more. Scientific respectability still eluded him. As the stories spread, and Mesmer's more and more fantastic claims reached the ears of his peers, those who had once merely laughed at his absurdities became more and more concerned about his irregularities. More and more his peers began to see him less as a misguided scientist and more as a charlatan and a fraud.

The whole affair came to a head when word began to leak out in the city of Paris that Mesmer was forming his own secret society—"The Society of Harmony"—to promote the use of animal magnetism for the "greater good of society." It was time, the French government decided, to look into Mesmer's claims.

The commission set up by the government began its investigation of Mesmer's theories in 1785. The group included such eminent personages as Benjamin Franklin, then living in France; Antoine Lavoisier, France's leading chemist; the astronomer Jean Sylvain Bailly; and Joseph Guillotin, for whom the guillotine was named.

The commission's final report, immaculately detailed and submitted after exhaustive investigations, devastated Mesmer and ruined his reputation in Paris. There was absolutely no evidence for the existence of "animal magnetism," the commission concluded. All the supposed "cures" and effects claimed for its existence could be attributed to the stimulated imaginations of Mesmer's clients and patients. In short "animal magnetism" did not exist. What did exist was a commanding and strong-willed practitioner whose "suggestions" triggered appropriate responses in his patients.

Mesmer's days of glory were over. Returning to Vienna a ridiculed but wealthy man, he insisted until the end of his life that he had been ruined by jealous rivals who disdained his scientific achievements and his important discovery of a new and powerful force in the universe.

Medical quacks and charlatans of all kinds flourished in the 18th century. Given the antics of Mesmer and others like him, it is not surprising that some historians have called the 18th century the "golden age of quackery," existing side by side with some of the greatest advances of science in history. Writing in 1710 about the many quacks in the streets of London and quoted in C. J. S. Thompson's *The Quacks of Old London,* Joseph Addison made these comments: "If a man has pains in his head, colics in his bowels, or spots on his clothes, he may meet with proper cures and remedies. If a man would recover a wife, or a horse that is stolen or strayed, if he wants new sermons, electuaries, asses' milk or anything else for his body or his mind this is the place to look for them."

Like many of the medical quacks of our own age, the pseudoscientists of the 1700s were quick to adorn their folk medicines and "cures" with the trappings of science. One of these, a man who called himself Katterfelto, traveled in a large caravan accompanied with an assortment of black cats and, according to his advertising, his very own "newly invented Solar Microscope." Through this marvelous device, according to an article of the time, one could see ". . . insects on the hedges . . . larger than ever, and those insects which caused the late influenza will be seen as large as birds, and in a drop of water the size of a pins head there will be seen above 50,000 insects; the same in beer, milk, vinegar, flour, blood, cheese, etc. . . ."

After using his exciting "solar microscope" for a lure, Katterfelto proceeded to sell his willing audiences the magical "Dr. Blato's medicines," which promised to cure a wide variety of ills. Obviously a man who liked to satisfy all of his customers, the good doctor, along with his lectures on "natural science" and medicine, also expounded on the arts of dice, cards, and billiards.

Although Addison was fascinated with the many quacks practicing their trades in the London streets, like Paris, London also had more than its share of charlatans and pseudoscientists working their trade amongst the upper classes. One of the most notorious of these, James Graham, operated in one of the city's wealthiest districts. Graham, born in England in 1745, immigrated to America in his youth. It was while living in Philadelphia that he became aware of Benjamin Franklin's experiments with electricity. Returning to

London in 1775, Graham immediately began promoting his wonderful new "electric medicine." With electricity all the vogue, Graham soon found himself inundated with clients.

Graham's treatments, which he claimed would cure all and any illnesses brought to him, consisted of administering sudden jolts of electricity to his patients by means of an electrical crown. Perhaps as much for the titillation and novelty of the experience as for its supposed medical efficiency, people paid handsomely for the treatment, and Graham soon found himself a wealthy man. His next move was to establish a much larger operation, which he called "The Temple of Health." Opening the "temple" in 1779, Graham treated his ever-broadening group of clients to a wide variety of marvels. In the opulent rooms of the temple, the wealthy and the privileged could treat themselves not only to Graham's lectures on the wondrous effects of his electrical medicine but could also try out his treatments, lying on lush couches and enjoying the enchantment of semi-nude dancing women.

Graham's most favored device, though, was his famous "Celestial Bed." Housed in one of the most lavish rooms in the temple, the bed was 12 feet long by 9 feet wide and could be tilted at different angles. Surrounded by soft music and overhung with a large mirror, loving couples—after paying a large fee—could enjoy a night of bliss enhanced by jolts of electricity issuing from the bed's headboard. With the experience thus enhanced by this "electrical fluid," the hopeful lovers, Graham claimed, would be "blessed with progeny."

With the growing understanding that wisdom and knowledge was no longer the sole province of the churches, the privileged and the elite began to encounter a large cadre of such pretenders. For each true follower of Copernicus, Galileo, and Newton who labored to unravel the secrets of nature in their laboratories, a hundred more sold seemingly marvelous revelations and "discoveries," both in the streets and among the sensation-seeking elite. With the shackles of authority beginning to break all around them, a bewildered public became bedazzled by the changes. For the first time in their lives, many of them began to recognize the existence of possibilities. For the vast majority, ignorant of the scientific method but learning of the wonders of scientific results, it began to seem that perhaps after all anything was possible. If Franklin, why not Mesmer or Graham? If Newton could explain the motions of the planets, who was to say then that Cagliostro could not also explain the motions of a human being's future?

As the seeds of the Scientific Revolution began to bear fruit in the 18th century, it seemed to many that perhaps no fruit after all was forbidden, or at least nothing was impossible. If the secrets of nature could indeed be unlocked, might not it then be possible that within those secrets lay things even beyond the probing of science itself?

Ironically then, the age that hoped to see reason and the scientific method dispel the ancient scourges of superstition gave birth itself to a newly fortified superstition, one in which the workings of nature replaced the workings of gods and demons to produce the supernatural effects that so much of humankind still yearned for.

Ironically, too, this "natural supernaturalism" remains as one of the 18th century's darker legacies to the world of the 21st century.

Conclusion
Beginnings of a Counter-Revolution

FOR MANY HISTORIANS THE PERIOD of the Enlightenment came to an end between 1776 (at the time of the American Declaration of Independence) and 1789 (with the fall of the Bastille and the beginning of the French Revolution). Even before these dramatic events, however, a reaction had begun slowly to erode the reign of Enlightenment ideals of rational and scientific philosophy. Not everyone had embraced the doctrine of reason. Some thinkers, among them Jean-Jacques Rousseau, detested and feared both science and newly developing technologies and looked for "enlightenment" through the exploration of feelings and emotions. Faith and the experience of the senses were all one needed to understand the fundamental truths of life and to live ethically.

Still others, including the German author and philosopher Johann Wolfgang von Goethe, composed cautionary books, plays, and essays against what they viewed as the arrogance and sterility of the new scientific viewpoint. Feeling that science had robbed both nature and humans of much of their beauty and spiritual values, many people began to turn toward other paths to "truths." Some, like Goethe and the German school of *Naturphilosophie*, preferred to take a more romanticized and "holistic" view of nature, a view sentimentalized and romanticized in England and France by a group of writers and artists called the romantics. Others, feeling that religion itself was in danger of being corrupted by its accommodation to some of the new scientific methods, turned back to a more traditional approach to the Bible and its teachings.

But, despite this backlash in the arts and religion toward the end of the century, the influence of the scientific method had stimulated productive and positive lines of thought in every area of life,

176

from government to industry, and from psychology and education to philosophy.

Sturm und Drang

The German expression *Sturm und Drang* (storm and stress) captures the sense of revolt in late 18th-century literary circles against the discipline required by scientific methods, rational thinking, what began to be seen as the "cult" of Enlightenment ideals, rigidity, and sterility. As this precursor to romanticism began to take shape, literary wellsprings were seen to be nurtured by nature, intuition, individual genius, fancy, emotion, and impulse. It was the beginning of a nearly spontaneous shift of mindset that would eventually envelope most of Europe, but especially France, Germany, and England. It was as if a giant pendulum had begun to swing in a different direction. In Germany both the poet and dramatist Friederich von Schiller and Goethe began their careers as active participants in the Sturm und Drang movement.

Born in 1749 in Frankfurt am Main, Germany, Goethe began his university studies at 16 in Leipzig, where he wrote his first poetry and plays. Later he studied at Strassburg, where he met the philosopher and literary critic Johann Gottfried von Herder, who helped lay the foundation for Goethe's early involvement with Sturm und Drang.

Herder introduced Goethe to the sweeping beauty of Gothic architecture, the lyricism of German folk music, and the wide-ranging, non-classical works of William Shakespeare. Goethe drank in the richness of this cultural education and applied his versatile talent to his first novel, *Die Leiden des jungen Werthers* (*The Sorrows of Young Werther*), published in 1774. This celebration of individualism and the novel's style recalls the sentimental novels of Jean-Jacques Rousseau, and the hero, young Werther, became the epitome of the

Johann Wolfgang von Goethe, scientist, poet, dramatist, novelist, and early leader of the romantic movement (*Culver Pictures*)

ideal romantic hero. For Goethe, though, Sturm und Drang was a passage of youth. He would go on to write his epic *Faust* and to make contributions to the science of biology and science history. Critics usually see both Goethe and Schiller as classicists, not romantics.

For others Sturm und Drang was the bridge to another world, the world of romanticism—a profound wave that was not so much a cogent philosophy as it was an intentional counterpoint to, even a negation of, the Enlightenment. Where the Enlightenment celebrated science and its processes and

Jean-Jacques Rousseau's celebration of the individual and attraction to sensibility over reason formed the cornerstone of the romantic movement that evolved in the early 19th century. *(Stock Montage, Inc.)*

methods, romanticism shunned science. Where the Enlightenment was cosmopolitan, romanticism celebrated what we would call "roots," such as folk music and folktales. The fundamental grounding of romanticism lay in individual differences, not uniformity; in individual experience, including nationality.

The development of the movement differed from country to country. In England it was a response to the French Revolution, a reaction on the part of the early romantic poets William Blake, Wordsworth, and Coleridge to the Reign of Terror that took place in France following the Revolution. The lyric poetry of these three romantics became the hallmark of the movement there.

In Germany, Herder embraced romanticism as a rejection of French intellectual models and an embrace of the homeland of Germany.

Despite being the working home of Swiss-born Jean-Jacques Rousseau and the site of the political events that helped spur the development of romanticism, the strength of the Enlightenment in France delayed the Gallic entry into romanticism until 1830 or 1840.

As the role model for "Enlightenment government," with all the recommended checks and balances and well-reasoned structure, the United States missed out on the romantic movement almost entirely.

While pride of national origin and individualism both can be beneficial, the sacking of science and reason is, well, illogical. With the possible exception of Henry David Thoreau, which of the naysayers against technology, science, and reason would wish to give up the improvements these human gifts have brought to their lives? Even Thoreau was known to put on his hiking shoes and head for the home of a bountiful neighbor when he needed the taste of good home cooking accomplished with all the amenities of a real kitchen.

The human animal has many facets, and room must be made for as much human diversity as possible—therein lies the greatest potential for human development. Not everyone must be a scientist. Sensibility, nature, and the individual's right to be different are all vitally important to human endeavour. But stereotyping science and forgetting the gifts afforded by science and the applications of well-reasoned thought amount to cultural suicide.

The fate of science and its continued revelations of the facts beneath the mysteries of nature would see some rough seas ahead during the years of romanticism. Yet the 19th century also held great promise for science—a time of great change and exciting discoveries. It would be a time of discoveries about human lineage that would change fundamentally the way humans see themselves; discoveries about geology that would change our understanding of the planet we live on; and insights about physics, chemistry, and astronomy that would change the way we thought about the universe and how it works. The days to come would bring both epiphanies of understanding and perplexing conflicts of old ideas with new information—the ever-changing, self-correcting human wonder that we call science.

CHRONOLOGY

The 18th Century

1642

▶ Disagreements between Charles I and Parliament lead to the English Civil War

1643

▶ Louis XIV becomes king of France

1649

▶ King Charles I of England is executed

1654

▶ Bishop James Ussher (1581–1656) publishes his argument based on biblical chronology that Earth was created by God on October 26, 4004 B.C.E. at 9:00 A.M.
▶ The Black Death strikes eastern Europe

1662

▶ The Royal Society is founded in England

1666

▶ Paris Academy of Sciences founded

1676–78

▸ Edmond Halley charts stars in the Southern Hemisphere

1687

▸ Isaac Newton's *Principia mathematica* is published

1689

▸ The English Parliament passes the Bill of Rights

1690

▸ John Locke publishes his *Essay Concerning Human Understanding*

1691

▸ Thomas Burnet publishes his "Sacred Theory of the Earth," an attempt to reconcile his belief in Newton's new "natural causes" philosophy with traditional biblical belief

1695

▸ John Woodward's "Essay Towards a Natural History of the Earth" is published. Woodward believes fossils to be the remains of living things but attributes their demise to the biblical flood

1698

▸ Sailing aboard the ship *Paramour Pink,* Edmund Halley begins first ocean voyage devoted solely to scientific research

1700

▸ With a population of about 550,000, London is the largest city in Europe

1704

▸ Newton's *Opticks* is published

1705

▸ Halley predicts the return in 1758 of the comet that will eventually be called Halley's Comet

1709

▶ New techniques in producing iron, which would be used in manufacturing better machinery, are developed in England, setting the stage for the Industrial Revolution

1718

▶ Halley discovers proper motion of the stars

1727

▶ James Bradley explains the aberration of the stars, linking it to the Earth's motion
▶ Stephen Hales publishes his work on plants and air, *Vegetable Staticks*

1733

▶ John Kay patents the so-called flying shuttle, a breakthrough in weaving, in England

1733–37

▶ Charles Dufay begins publishing six memoirs on electricity

1735

▶ Carolus Linnaeus's *Systema naturae* (System of nature)—his system of classification of organisms—is published

1736

▶ Pierre de Maupertuis leads an expedition to Lapland to measure the length of a degree; proves Earth is flattened at poles

1737

▶ Calcutta earthquake kills 300,000

1738

▶ Daniel Bernoulli's *Hydrodynamica* is published, explaining the relationship between the pressure and velocity of fluids, now known as the Bernoulli effect

> Maupertuis publishes results of his expedition, which support Newton's theory about the shape of the Earth
> Voltaire's *Eléments de la philosophie de Newton* is published

1739

> Royal Society of Edinburgh founded (receiving a charter in 1738); scientific society founded also in Stockholm, later called Kungliga Svenska Vetenskapsakademien

1739–40

> David Hume, Scottish philosopher, publishes *A Treatise of Human Nature*, in which he tries to apply experimental method to human psychology

1742

> Royal Danish Academy of Sciences and Letters is founded
> Anders Celsius invents the Celsius temperature scale

1743

> Benjamin Franklin helps establish the American Philosophical Society at Philadelphia
> Jean d'Alembert publishes *Traité de dynamique* (Treatise on dynamics), expanding on Newton's law of motion

1744

> Maupertuis formulates principle of "least action" in physics

1745

> Buffon proposes that the Earth formed when a comet collided with the Sun

1746

> Denis Diderot publishes *Pensées philosophiques*, postulating that the presence of order in nature proves the existence of God
> Leonhard Euler works out the mathematics of the refraction of light
> Leyden jar invented, facilitating the study of electricity

1747

▶ Jean d'Alembert presents first general use of partial differential equations in mathematical physics

1748

▶ Mikhail Lomonosov formulates the laws of conservation of mass and energy
▶ Julien de La Mettrie publishes *L'homme machine*, describing humans as machines without free will
▶ John Needham and Buffon think they prove spontaneous generation exists

1749

▶ Buffon formulates modern definition of species and publishes his *Théorie de la terre* (Theory of the Earth) in the first volume of his *Histoire naturelle*, a 55-year, 44-volume project that popularizes the study of nature
▶ Denis Diderot publishes *Lettre sur les aveugles* (Letter on the blind), setting forth ideas about materialism, human dependence on the senses, and his theory of variability and adaptation
▶ Emilie du Châtelet completes translation of Newton's *Principia* into French from Latin. It is published in 1759 with a preface by Voltaire and becomes widely influential

1750

▶ Thomas Wright publishes *An Original Theory and New Hypothesis of the Universe*

1750–60

▶ Approximate beginning of the Industrial Revolution in England

1751

▶ First volume of the *Encyclopédie* is published; last volume published 1772, for a total 17 volumes of articles and 11 of illustrations; five supplementary volumes follow in 1776–77
▶ Benjamin Franklin publishes *Experiments and Observations on Electricity*

▶ Carolus Linnaeus publishes *Philosophia botanica* (Botanical philosophy)
▶ Pierre de Maupertuis publishes *Système de la nature* (System of nature), theoretical speculation on heredity and the origin of species by chance

1752

▶ Benjamin Franklin's kite experiment
▶ Jean Guettard publishes short booklet explaining his ideas about geology and rock strata

1753

▶ Carolus Linnaeus publishes *Species plantarum* (Species of plants)
▶ British Museum chartered
▶ Immanuel Kant formulates ideas on evolution of the universe from primeval nebulae

1754

▶ Charles Bonnet publishes *Recherches sur l'usage des feuilles des plantes* (On nutritional value of plants); Etienne Bonnet publishes *Traité de sensations* (Treatise on the Senses), claiming that knowledge only reaches us through the senses

1755

▶ Kant formulates dust-cloud theory of origin of solar system and proposes that nebulae are star systems like the Milky Way in his *Allegemeine Naturgeschichte und Theorie des Himmels* (*Universal Natural History and Theory of the Heavens*)
▶ Earthquake in northern Persia kills 40,000, and Lisbon earthquake kills 60,000

1756

▶ Joseph Black publishes *Experiments upon Magnesia,* first detailed account of chemical action and the first work of quantitative chemistry
▶ Voltaire's "Essay on the Customs and Manners of Nations" published

1759

‣ Caspar Friedrich Wolff publishes *Theoria generations* (Theory of generation), refuting homunculus theory

1760

‣ Giovanni Morgagni establishes pathology as a science

1760s

‣ James Cook surveys coasts of Labrador and Newfoundland; first of scientific navigators; three scientific voyages to Pacific: 1768–71, 1772–75, and 1776–79

1761

‣ Joseph Black discovers latent heat
‣ Giovanni Morgagni does first important work in pathological anatomy (on the causes of diseases)

1762

‣ James Bradley compiles new star catalog of 60,000 stars
‣ Catherine II the Great becomes ruler of Russia

1764

‣ Voltaire publishes *Dictionnaire philosophique,* argues against the Great Chain of Being
‣ Charles Bonnet develops preformation theory

ca. 1766

‣ Lunar Society founded in England. It is a private group that draws members from both science and industry
‣ Solar eclipse observed by James Cook during his survey of the coast of Newfoundland
‣ Cavendish announces his work on hydrogen to the Royal Society (discovery of hydrogen)
‣ Joseph Priestley meets Benjamin Franklin in London

1767

‣ Priestley publishes *History of Electricity*

1768–71

▶ First of James Cook's voyages to the Pacific

1769

▶ James Watt invents the first practical steam engine
▶ Worldwide observations of the second transit of Venus of the century

1770

▶ In America, British soldiers fire on colonists in the Boston Massacre. The population in the American colonies is now nearly 2.2 million

1772–75

▶ Cook's second voyage to the Pacific

1773

▶ Karl Wilhelm Scheele discovers oxygen a year before Priestley does, but the work is not published until 1777
▶ Boston Tea Party: Angry American colonists dump British tea into Boston waters in an act of rebellion

1774

▶ Priestley discovers oxygen (actually Scheele isolated it first but did not publish the discovery)

1775

▶ Beginning of the American Revolution

1776

▶ American Declaration of Independence signed; Revolution continues. The largest city in America, Philadelphia, now has a population of nearly 40,000

1776–79

▶ Cook's third and last voyage to the Pacific

1777

▶ Scheele publishes *A Chemical Treatise on Air and Fire,* describing his discovery of oxygen

1779

▶ Lavoisier names oxygen

1781

▶ Charles Messier compiles a catalog of more than 100 nebulae
▶ James Watt, who has learned a great deal about heat from a friend, chemist Joseph Black, perfects his steam engine. It is another major step in the Industrial Revolution
▶ William Herschel discovers Uranus

1782

▶ John Goodricke announces his observations of a "variable" star, Algol
▶ Oliver Evans works on an early version of a locomotive

1783

▶ The American Revolution ends and Great Britain recognizes the independence of the United States

1783–84

▶ Henry Cavendish demonstrates that when hydrogen burns, it produces water, proving that water is a combination of two gases, not itself an element as thought by the Greeks

1784

▶ James Watt patents a locomotive two years after Oliver Evans had patented a similar device

1784–89

▶ Charles-Augustin de Coulomb writes his memoirs on electricity and magnetism

1785

▶ Cavendish finds evidence of the existence of argon (confirmed in following century by Ramsay)

1786

▶ Lavoisier names hydrogen (discovered by Cavendish 20 years earlier)

1787

▶ Abraham Werner, primarily a teacher of great influence, publishes a 28-page booklet outlining his ideas

1788

▶ James Hutton first publishes his theory of Earth in the Royal Society of Edinburgh's *Transactions*

1789

▶ Antoine Lavoisier publishes *Traité élémentaire de chimie*
▶ Enraged French citizens attack the Paris prison known as the Bastille, marking the beginning of the French Revolution

1791

▶ Luigi Galvani publishes *De viribus electricitatis in motu musculari commentarius*

1793

▶ In America the inventor Eli Whitney invents the cotton gin
▶ Louis XVI is executed: Reign of Terror begins in France, lasting for two violent and bloody years

1794

▶ Lavoisier executed
▶ In England rioters, afraid that the violence of the French Revolution will strike their country, attack supporters of the French revolutionaries, including Joseph Priestley, an outspoken supporter of the revolution, and he flees to the United States

1795

- A new French constitution establishes the Directory
- Hutton publishes his theory with new materials in two volumes titled *Theory of the Earth*
- Georges Cuvier appointed assistant to the professor of comparative anatomy at the Museum of Natural History in Paris

1796

- Pierre-Simon Laplace proposes the nebular hypothesis
- English physician Edward Jenner pioneers the use of vaccination against smallpox

1798

- Benjamin Thompson (Count Rumford) publishes his *Experimental Inquiry Concerning the Source of Heat Excited by Friction*
- Jenner publishes *An Inquiry into the Causes and Effects of the Variolae Vaccinae*
- Eli Whitney builds a factory in New Haven, Connecticut, to mass-produce firearms

1799

- Alessandro Volta sends his famous letter to the president of the Royal Society, Joseph Banks, titled, "On the electricity excited by the mere contact of conducting substances of different kinds"
- Napoléon Bonaparte seizes power in France

1800

- Cuvier publishes his *Leçons d'anatomie comparée* (Lessons on comparative anatomy)
- Herschel builds 40-foot-long reflecting telescope

GLOSSARY

astronomical unit (AU)   The distance from Earth to the Sun, 93 million miles, often used as a unit of measurement in astronomy

atom   Leucippus (Greece, eighth century B.C.E.) said atoms were the smallest indivisible unit of matter, differing only in shape and size. Today's ideas about atoms originate from models developed by Ernest Rutherford and Niels Bohr

caloric   Term used in the 18th century to describe heat seen as a fluid, used by Lavoisier and others

calx   Oxide (18th-century term)

catastrophist geology   The school of thought that the Earth's geological features were the product of sudden, catastrophic events, such as floods, earthquakes, and volcanoes (compare *uniformitarian geology*)

chemistry   Today the scientific study of the composition, structure, properties, and reactions of matter, especially at the level of atomic and molecular systems. In the 18th century, the study of mixtures of substances and the results of changing the temperature of substances (compare *physics*)

dephlogisticated air   Oxygen (term used by Joseph Priestley in the 18th century)

element   Defined in 1787 by Antoine Lavoisier as a substance that is chemically "simple," in other words, one that cannot be further decomposed

epigenesis   Series of distinct phases through which an embryo passes

fixed air   Eighteenth-century term for carbon dioxide

galaxy   A large groups of stars, cosmic dust, and gas bound together by gravitation into an astronomical system

gravity   The natural force that makes objects having mass attract each other

nebula (plural: nebulae)   A large cloud of interstellar gas and dust; the term originally was used for any object in the heavens that appeared fuzzy through the telescope

nebular hypothesis   An early theory of the origin of the solar system (Kant, Laplace) that proposed it was formed from a cloud of material collapsing under the effects of gravitation

Neptunism   Theory of geology that holds that all rocks are laid down by water and sediment (compare *Plutonism*)

parallax   An apparent shift in position of an object viewed from two different locations, for example, from the Earth at two different positions on opposite sides of its orbit (achieved by observing the objects at six-month intervals). The greater the apparent change in position, or annual parallax, the nearer the star

periodical   Occurring at regular intervals, having periods or repeated cycles

philosophe   French for "philosopher." A writer and intellectual of the 18th-century Englightenment in France

phlogiston   According to 18th-century belief, one of three varieties of "earth," a combustible material lost when a substance burns

physics   The scientific study of matter and energy, and the interactions between them; originally the study of all natural things (compare *chemistry*)

Plutonism   The theory, common in 1880, that the origin and nature of all rocks (and thus, the crust of the Earth) is explainable by the effects of heat (compare *Neptunism*)

teleology   Use of predetermined purpose to explain the universe; the idea that future events control the present, that is, that "A is so in order that B might be so," that nature or natural processes are directed toward an end or shaped by a purpose

triangulation   A system used to measure distance through the use of known facts about the relationship of angles and distances in triangles

uniformitarian geology   The school of thought that held that geological features are the product of natural forces operating steadily and slowly over long periods of time (compare *catastrophist geology*)

FURTHER READING AND WEB SITES

About Science in General

Cole, K. C. *First You Build a Cloud: And Other Reflections on Physics as a Way of Life.* San Diego, Calif.: Harvest Books, 1999. Well-written, lively look at physics, presented in a thoughtful and insightful way by a writer who cares for her subject.

Ferris, Timothy, ed. *The World Treasury of Physics, Astronomy and Mathematics.* New York: Little, Brown, 1991. Anthology of mostly modern physics but includes some general papers on the philosophy of science, as well as some delightful poetry on physics. Sometimes difficult but well worth browsing through.

Gonick, Larry, and Art Huffman. *The Cartoon Guide to Physics.* New York: Harper Perennial, 1991. Fun, but the whiz-bang approach sometimes zips by important points a little too fast.

Hann, Judith. *How Science Works.* Pleasantville, N.Y.: Reader's Digest, 1991. Lively, well-illustrated book on physics for young readers. Good, brief explanations of basic laws and short historical overviews accompany many easy experiments readers can perform.

Hazen, Robert M., and James Trefil. *Science Matters: Achieving Scientific Literacy.* New York: Doubleday, 1991. A clear and readable overview of basic principles of science and how they apply in today's world.

Holzinger, Philip R. *House of Science.* New York: John Wiley & Sons, 1990. Lively question-and-answer discussion of science for young adults. Includes activities and experiments.

Rensberger, Boyce. *How the World Works: A Guide to Science's Greatest Discoveries.* New York: William Morrow, 1987. Lucid and readable explanations of major scientific concepts, terms explained in A-to-Z format, and excellent discussions of the scientific method and how science works.

Trefil, James. *1001 Things Everyone Should Know about Science.* New York: Doubleday, 1992. Just what the title says—and well done.

About the History of Science in the 18th Century

Brock, William H. *The Chemical Tree: A History of Chemistry.* Norton History of Science, Roy Porter, ed. New York: W. W. Norton and Co., 1993. Includes the 18th-century pursuit of the chemistry of air.

Brooke, John Hedley. *Science and Religion: Some Historical Perspectives.* Cambridge: Cambridge University Press, 1991. This higher-level book is sometimes difficult, but it gives a well-presented and insightful look at the relationship between science and religion throughout history.

Corben, Herbert C. *The Struggle to Understand: A History of Human Wonder and Discovery.* Buffalo, N.Y.: Prometheus Books, 1991. Explores the history of scientific discovery and superstition and supernaturalism from prehistoric times to the present.

Eighteenth-Century Resources. Links to general 18th-century historical resources on the Internet, covering the social, political, and intellectual climate of the time. Available online. URL: http://newark.rutgers. edu/~jlynch/18th/history.html. Accessed June 23, 2003.

The Enlightenment, the Age of Exploration, the Age of Reason, and the Scientific Revolution: A Guide to Resources and Research on the Web. Available online. URL: http://web.uccs.edu/~history/index/enlightenment. html. Accessed June 23, 2003.

Gould, Stephen Jay. *The Flamingo's Smiling.* New York: W. W. Norton and Company, 1985. The always readable Gould here includes chapters on the Great Chain of Being and the ideas and work of Maupertuis, along with other assorted essays on natural history and evolutionary theory.

———. *Hen's Teeth and Horse's Toes.* New York: W. W. Norton and Co., 1983. Has a good chapter on Hutton and his ideas. Also chapters on Cuvier and early geography.

Horvitz, Leslie Alan. *Eureka! Scientific Breakthroughs that Changed the World.* New York: John Wiley & Sons, 2002. Covers Joseph Priestley and the discovery of oxygen.

Internet History of Science Sourcebook. Available online. URL: http://www. fordham.edu/halsall/science/sciencesbook.html. Accessed June 23, 2003.

Internet Scientific Revolution Sourcebook. Available online. URL: http://www. fordham.edu/halsall/mod/modsbook09.html. Accessed June 23, 2003.

Major Scientific & Medical Discoveries, Inventions & Events, 1650–1800. Available online. URL: http://www.sonoma.edu/history/reason/science.html. Accessed June 23, 2003.

Milner, Richard. *The Encyclopedia of Evolution: Humanity's Search for Its Origins*. New York: Facts On File, 1990. Engrossing for hunting facts or browsing, one of the few books of its kind that is also completely rewarding, entertaining, and informative as just plain reading.

Porter, Roy, ed. *The Cambridge Illustrated History of Medicine*. Cambridge, Mass.: Cambridge University Press, 2001. In essays written by experts in the field, this illustrated history traces the evolution of medicine from the contributions made by early Greek physicians through the Renaissance, Scientific Revolution, and 19th and 20th centuries up to current advances. Sidebars cover parallel social or political events and certain diseases.

Silver, Brian L. *The Ascent of Science*. New York: Oxford University Press, 1998. A sweeping overview of the history of science from the Renaissance to the present.

timelinescience: one thousand years of scientific thought. National Grid for Learning (NGfl, British Educational Communications and Technology Agency). Available online. URL: http://www.timelinescience.org. Accessed June 23, 2003.

About Scientists

Brown, G. I. *Scientist, Statesman, Soldier, Spy: Count Rumford*. Paperback edition. London: Sutton Publishing, 2002. Details the extraordinary life of this remarkable American scientific genius.

Isaacson, Walter. *Benjamin Franklin: An American Life*. New York: Simon & Schuster, 2003. A readable, highly detailed account that explores each of Franklin's remarkable accomplishments in depth.

Meadows, Jack. *The Great Scientists*. Reissue edition. New York: Oxford University Press, 1993. Easy-to-read, well-presented, and nicely illustrated history of science. Includes coverage of Lavoisier.

Morgan, Edmund S. *Benjamin Franklin*. New Haven, Conn.: Yale University Press, 2002. An excellent short biography that explores the many sides of this versatile scientist-statesman-celebrity-author.

INDEX

DATE DUE

FOLLETT